The Abingdon Religious Education Monographs

John W. Langdale, General Editor

GEORGE HERBERT BETTS, Editor

JESUS IN OUR TEACHING

CLARENCE TUCKER CRAIG

Professor of New Testament Language and Literature
Oberlin Graduate School of Theology

THE ABINGDON PRESS

NEW YORK   CINCINNATI   CHICAGO

DEDICATED TO THE MEMORY OF
MY FATHER
FROM WHOM I FIRST LEARNED THE PLACE OF
JESUS IN OUR TEACHING

CONTENTS

PREFACE

Books about Jesus are so numerous that one might be expected to apologize for offering another. I know, however, of none that adopts the approach followed in this little volume. The life and teaching of Jesus have been recounted many times. There are many inspirational volumes about Jesus, but few of them are controlled by the historic picture of Jesus. It is my conviction that Jesus himself is of fundamental significance; not a Jesus of dogmatic theology nor some modernized creation of contemporary piety, but the historic Jesus of Nazareth. We do not yet possess adequate treatments of his place in our teaching.

The aim of this book is to state in brief compass the present status of the research about Jesus and then to provide some suggestions in the practical use of those results. It attempts to offer a bridge between the work of New Testament scholars on the one hand and workers in the field of religious education on the other. The former necessarily pursue their studies in an atmosphere of academic detachment, while the latter are often so busy perfecting their techniques that they do not have time to master the content of the religion they would cultivate.

This essay is not intended as a textbook to awaken interest in Jesus. Relatively too much space had to be given to the problems involved to achieve the other end with any success. It is hoped, however, that it will bring church-school workers face to face with the essential issues in interpreting the real Jesus. Adequate texts are not yet available for most ages, and if they were, they could not be used in many of our churches. While a historical view of the Old Testament has permeated widely, the same cannot be said for the New Testament. There is much pioneering yet to be done, and much misunderstanding to be undergone before even the leadership of our churches comes to an accurate understanding of the beginnings of our religion.

Doubtless certain positions assumed in this book will appear new and startling to some readers. There is only one point of view, however, that will have novelty for scholars acquainted with the field. That is the working out of the relationship between ethics and eschatology. My study of the field has confirmed only more strongly than ever the conclusions first reached ten years ago. I believe that the position adopted is essentially conservative rather than radical on this point.

It is with a full sense of its inadequacy that this little book is sent forth. No one can be satisfied with his attempt to state what Jesus means. The endeavor throughout has been not to provide homiletic inspiration but to guide discriminating thinking. Hence, the enthusiasm of the author may not appear on the pages as forcefully as he would desire. The libraries are now full of impassioned tributes which bear testimony to the undying attraction of the Nazarene. There should likewise be a place for the more dispassionate analysis of the basis for these appreciations.

Our hope is that the educators who are qualified for the work will in the next few years provide us with the two types of texts called for in Chapter V. In the meanwhile ministers have a long task in educating congregations to accept a sincere historical approach to the understanding of the creative period of our religion.

I wish to thank the editor of this series, Dr. G. H. Betts, for his invaluable counsel and helpful suggestions, and my wife for her painstaking assistance at many stages in the preparation of the manuscript.

CLARENCE TUCKER CRAIG.

Oberlin, Ohio.

CHAPTER I

THE DILEMMA OF THE RELIGIOUS EDUCATOR

JESUS OF NAZARETH commands the attention of almost the entire world. It is in him rather than in Christianity that men are interested, for that name is linked with the exploitive policies of Western civilization. It is not the church, with its stuffy traditionalism and divisive organization, that appeals to men, but the Galilæan who would hardly recognize many of the ceremonies carried on in his name. Labor leaders who hurl anathemas at institutionalized religion speak of "Comrade Jesus," a member of the world's disinherited proletariat. "No one else is seriously bidding for the heart of the world," is the striking conclusion reported from an Indian religious leader.

Religious workers in sophisticated university circles would doubtless dispute the fact that the name of Jesus is hailed with universal acclamation. They find that it often produces a barrier rather than commends an insight to claim his authority. Various explanations may be suggested to account for this fact. It may be that the name of Jesus is so indissolubly linked up with outworn, unscientific, and rejected presentations of religion that he is a hindrance rather than a help to a fresh approach to the religious problem. They at once think of Jesus in terms of ideas which they have repudiated, and have no desire to reconsider this "mind-set."

The reforms in the field of religious education during the past twenty-five years have transformed many of the old Bible schools into church schools. In conformity to newer philosophies of education, the aim is no longer described as that of transmitting a fixed body of information from a library of religious literature. Rather, the experience of the children is made central in a developmental process. The Bible is now looked upon simply as one of the means to be used in the attainment of this life goal of transforming character. Differences of opinion still exist as to what materials and methods are most valuable in attaining the desired ends. There is likewise disagreement on what constitutes the Christian experience we seek to develop. For some it is a pattern definitely transmitted from the past. Others emphasize the belief that Christian experience must be dynamic and creative. We do not know the goals which we should pursue, but must discover them experimentally. We should not seek to fit youth into our approved patterns, but should guide their discoveries.

However, few of the present college generation developed their experience of religion under the "new religious education." It is a Jesus embedded in outworn theologies that they hazily recall, and to which they remain indifferent and hostile. The modern religious educators of all schools believe that the real Jesus must become a part of the experience of our young people. Some relationship to him is presupposed in Christian character. Though it may be an exaggeration to say, with the representatives of the missionary movement of Jerusalem in 1928, "Jesus is our message," he is so significant a part of our message that he cannot be omitted from the education of any Christian youth. The International Council of Religious Education formulates as the second of the objectives of Christian education that it "seeks to develop in growing persons such an understanding and appreciation of the personality, life, and teachings of Jesus as will lead to experience of him as Saviour and Lord, loyalty to him and his cause, and will manifest itself in daily life and conduct."

The Jesus that concerns most modern educators is not the Christ of theology. The atoning significance of his death in the redemptive economy of God does not figure primarily in their texts. The sacramental Christ, and even the mystical "white companion," retreat into the background while the focus of attention rests upon the historical Man of Galilee. He is the one whose life we should imitate, whose way we should follow, and whose heroism should be our inspiration. We study the life of Jesus, not the speculative theologies of the church. We seek to stimulate an appreciation of his personality and an acceptance of his principles. "The Imitation of Christ" is the goal of much religious teaching, and for an increasing number represents the highest aim.

The Quest of the Real Jesus

But who was the Jesus of history? The average Bible reader assumes that to be a relatively easy question to answer. He reads the four Gospels and receives from them an overpowering series of impressions. He puts them together into a composite portrait. He probably reads one or more popular lives of Jesus which weave the Gospels together in harmonistic fashion, avoiding all puzzling questions. If his interest has been intrigued he probably absorbs the best sellers which seek to capitalize the modern interest in Jesus. If he reads more than one, and takes time to reflect, it may be somewhat puzzling.

One account will ooze with Latin sentimentality; another is just as full of Anglo-Saxon practicality. He may discover that the literary men who have made a business out of "debunking biographies" have been primarily concerned with adorning a good tale. Who is this Jesus of Nazareth?

Our average Bible reader may be dimly aware that for years scholars have been devoted to the task of distilling the picture of the historical Jesus. But he certainly has not read such a book as Schweitzer's *Quest of the Historical Jesus*, nor has he found that many of the scholarly reconstructions meet his needs. Something has been done in popularizing the main results in our best church-school helps. But the scholars with their never-ending investigation of problems do not furnish the sort of "cut-and-dried" results which the practical worker desires.

We ought to expect of our religious education "leaders" a deeper understanding of the problem than this. If Jesus is as important for the curriculum as they say he is, he ought to be worthy of their most intense study with all of the aids of critical historical scholarship. No one of them would dare neglect the mastery of his Dewey or Kilpatrick. But much of their writing reveals a pathetic ignorance of the contemporary study of Jesus. They seek through "modern methods" to obviate the necessity of seriously grappling with historical data.

It would lead us too far afield to recount here the various steps in recovering the historical portrait of Jesus. One charge which Schweitzer makes against the liberal German portrait of Jesus of the nineteenth century must be recorded. He claimed, and rightly so, that it was too modern. It was a pale reflection of the investigators themselves. They had not taken seriously enough the historical task of reconstructing the actual background of his life and thought-world. They had read modern meanings into gospel phrases. They had too naïvely assumed that Jesus must mean what they thought he should mean.

If such statements contain severe criticism of the work of those scholars, they are not exaggerated in describing the unauthentic Jesus which many religious educators imagine. We have sought a Jesus who would speak to us in our terms and who would fit into the modern world. We have not been interested in the "antiquarian lore of Palestine." We ask what Jesus has to say about modern issues, drawing upon farfetched analogies. We reject a historical interest in the problems which he actually faced, forgetting that we thereby forfeit any possibility of knowing what he actually tried to do.

The modern religious educator has rarely faced the frank question as to whether he really wanted to know the truth about Jesus. Following the bent of his "technique," he has looked for what he could "use." He combines his "problem-project approach" with "loyalty to Jesus" by presenting Jesus as the supreme problem-solver. As a matter of fact, the Jesus with whom he is dealing is little more than a symbol for his own religious idealism. The Jesus who is presented to students as the ideal is not the carefully sifted portrait given by historical criticism. He is a symbol for our own ideals.

A comparison of the practice with the professions of modern religious educators raises the very real question as to whether the Jesus of history has a place in religious education. Though they may say, "A systematic study

of the life of Jesus or of the problem of the future life may
at times be the best way in which life needs can be
served,"[1] in practice those times are rarely discovered.
Courses which set out on a scientific historical task are
branded as "material-centered." It may be that history,
even the life of Jesus, is not religious education, but in that
case it would be much more honest to stop assuming that
an unauthentic Jesus is the "solution of our problems."

There is a danger in committing ourselves too readily
to the assumption that, of course, the life of Jesus will
be central in our curriculum. When we start with that
assumption, we are in danger of being influenced in our
quest of the historical Jesus by the use we think we can
make of the results. For example, most American
Christians do not consider poverty a Christian ideal. If
the life of Jesus is to be determinative for our youth,
we shall be hesitant to admit in our study of Jesus that it
was his ideal. Or, we say, he must have accommodated
himself to the world views of his time, for such ideas are
obviously impossible for us to hold! Every scientist
knows that he must approach his subject matter without
bias and without previous conviction of the result to be
found. Such is the impartiality demanded of a historian.
But can the religious educator ever admit such an attitude?

CAN WE SERVE TWO MASTERS?

This brings us face to face with the dilemma of the
modern religious educator. His aim is to be scientific.
But he knows much more about scientific pedagogy than

---

[1] Vieth, P. H., *Teaching for Christian Living.* 1929. The Bethany
Press.

about historical science in so far as it concerns investigation of the Bible. He seeks to organize his teaching not around knowledge of fact in past history, but possible solutions to present life problems. The day of the use of the Bible as an arsenal of theological proof-texts is happily waning. It is not being displaced by a genuinely historical approach. The Bible is now combed by the religious educator for passages that will furnish proof-text solutions. The new method may have pedagogical advantages in its favor, but the historian knows that it can lead to just as arbitrary and misleading results as the theory of the Bible as an arsenal of dogmatic proof-texts. That does not lead to respect for the Bible for what it is, but leads only to disrepute when the student discovers that false hopes have been raised.

This may be illustrated on an unusual scale from the chapter entitled "The Jesus Stereotype" in one of the most brilliant indictments of modern liberal Christianity of recent years.[2] Doctor Barnes here professes the highest respect for the religious leadership of a group of foremost modernists, except in their reference to the authority of Jesus. He insists that their case would be much stronger with him and other moderns if they would advance it upon their own authority and not summon a distant figure such as Jesus. For, says Barnes, they do not really get their ideas from Jesus, but, under the influence of "the Jesus stereotype" which they have inherited, they ascribe their own judgments to him. As a matter of fact, believes Barnes, the historical Jesus is quite irrelevant for our time and should be left to the antiquarian scholars.

[2] Barnes, H. E., *The Twilight of Christianity*.

17

Certainly, the men cited by Barnes are fully capable of defending their own intellectual insight and veracity without any assistance. We are all governed to some degree by emotional attachments, not least of all, Barnes himself. But if he considers Jesus quite "irrelevant," it is not entirely explainable from his individual perverseness of judgment. Exaggerated and unhistorical claims *have* been made; false points of view *have* often been adopted. Seeing only this side, and having no personal inclination to look further, he dismisses Jesus as of no significance. Our fear is that thousands of others will do likewise, and that the net result of an indiscriminate exaltation of Jesus will be to deprive him of his rightful pre-eminence.

Many religious educators are quite unaware of such a peril. They are zealously endeavoring to serve two masters—educational technique and historical science. If we take the words of Jesus himself with much seriousness, we may well suspect that such a course is headed for shipwreck. It would be begging the question to fit the names of God and Mammon to our alternatives. But can such a clash be avoided? As a matter of fact, will a presentation of the Jesus of history always meet the needs of the modern educator in developing the highest religious character?

The presence of such a dilemma has not often enough been faced. The acuteness of the problem has been avoided because many religious educators are unaware of its existence, and most technical New Testament scholars have shown little interest in what children would make of their results. It is, however, the crucial problem for any volume that would discuss JESUS IN OUR

TEACHING. That has objectives in life. One of the most fundamental of those objectives is honesty. If that be the case, we must be absolutely honest in portraying what Jesus said and what he did, in so far as we are able to recover it.

That ought to be axiomatic. Unfortunately, such is not quite the case. There are still a few people who believe that honesty can be inculcated by the story of the boy Washington who could not deny that he had chopped down his father's cherry tree with his own little hatchet. Historians may be agreed that its only foundation lay in the imagination of the pious pastor, Weems. Still, some moralists would be willing to use it, provided boys and girls did not react unfavorably to such a stilted prig. Of course we would all agree that the most valuable stories are not necessarily those which relate actual fact. Who supposes that the story which Jesus told of the forgiving father in Luke 15. 11-35 actually happened? It is truth, not fact. But it is quite another matter to claim that such an incident did take place in the life of a well-known man when such was not the case.

If we seek to be genuinely honest in our presentation of the life of Jesus, how, then, can we neglect to evaluate critically the traditions that have come down to us? Naturally, the individual Bible reader is not in position to do so. The cumulative labors of generations of scholars have been dedicated to the recovery of the Jesus of history. There is no unanimous verdict upon many points. There is honest difference of opinion regarding many facts. As many points have been settled by increasing knowledge, so we may expect more to be removed from conjecture to the kind of certainty which is possible in historical investigation. Undoubtedly, there will always remain questions of interpretation upon which agreement will never be possible. But none of these uncertainties relieve us of the necessity to be honest.

This does not mean that living religion is supposed to feed from the crumbs that fall from the table of historical scholarship. Religious experience is direct and primary. It does not depend upon the record of past events, but upon repeatable experiences to-day. But because of that truth there must be no hazy confusion between the "living Christ of faith" and the historical Jesus. Our present mystical experience cannot tell us in detail any facts about who Jesus was. Our interests and predilections have nothing to do with it at all. Our information about Jesus can be gleaned only from the sources. We have a right to bring to them but one predisposition— that we will honestly be guided by what they have to tell us.

THE ROAD AHEAD

Our study, then, must begin with a brief consideration of the nature of the sources of our information about Jesus. Everything depends upon handling them aright. Then we are in position to reconstruct the portrait that emerges from a sympathetic evaluation of those sources. From such a portrait, certain problems will arise which will call for separate consideration, such as miracles, legends, etc., and especially the problem of the authority of this Jesus for the modern conscience and mind. Problems are presented not only by our facts but by our pupils. The truth about Jesus can be conveyed to various age groups only as it is adapted to their comprehension and needs. We must then consider certain representative textbooks now available, and the principles which should be followed in teaching the life of Jesus. Then and only then will we be in a position to raise the question concerning modern values in Jesus. When we know what he tried to do, we can ask what significance it has for us. Therefore we turn first of all to an evaluation of the sources.

CHAPTER II

THE PROBLEM OF THE SOURCES

JESUS wrote nothing which has been preserved for posterity. We have no contemporaneous, disinterested account of his ministry. The few references in later Latin and Jewish writings testify at best that such a character lived. For all real knowledge about Jesus we are dependent upon those followers who worshiped through him. It is probably due to this religious adoration of the heavenly Christ that Paul and the other apostolic authors furnish so little concrete information concerning the earthly life of Jesus. We are almost wholly dependent upon the books called Gospels for our knowledge of him.

The word "gospel" means "good news." It comes from the opening sentence in Mark, "The beginning of the gospel of Jesus Christ." The word soon came to be applied to the book containing the "good news." Though the story might be told according to various authors, there was but one gospel. There were many attempts in the second century to imitate the earlier books, but before the end of that century, a leading bishop, Irenæus of Lyons, affirmed that as there were four corners of the earth, and four principal winds, there could be but four Gospels. Modern scholars agree that little if any authentic information was added in the so-called apocryphal Gospels.

Bible readers should understand that the Gospels

present a distinct literary type. They do not belong to the category of historical literature, though, of course, they contain much that is history. Their purpose is to give an interpretation of the facts, to show that God has performed a great act in history. They are for the edification and instruction of believers, and to aid in the missionary propaganda. No pretense of that detached objectivity which is essential to historical science is made in any of the Gospels.

Nor can they be classified as biography. Materials were not available to recount any long chronological sequence revealing character development. It was not the human struggle of a man which they sought to depict. It was the appearance of the Son of God upon earth, and the redemption which had come to men in his death and resurrection. Countless books have borne the title, "Life of Christ," but we living in the twentieth century are quite unable to do what was impossible in our earliest sources. We can learn much about Jesus from the gospel story, but a connected account of his life cannot be told, for it is illumined in only a few places.

The writer concurs in the judgment of those scholars who believe that none of our Gospels was written by eyewitnesses of the ministry of Jesus. Luke definitely affirms that he is dependent upon his sources; Mark has at best a secondary relationship to Peter and thus to the original events; it will soon appear that it is impossible to sustain the tradition that the apostle Matthew wrote the first Gospel. Though a wide difference of opinion still exists as to the authorship of the fourth Gospel, the number who assign it to the apostle John is diminishing. Hence, the all-important question for the historian is the nature and the value of the sources which the evangelists used. By "sources" we mean written documents and also oral traditions transmitted by interested groups.

THE SYNOPTIC PROBLEM

A century of painstaking study has been given to the literary analysis of the first three Gospels. Certain facts are incontrovertible. Foremost among these is that Mark is the earliest Gospel and one of the sources used by both "Matthew" and "Luke." These three are commonly referred to as the synoptic Gospels. That Matthew uses Mark is seen from the fact that he incorporates all but fifty-five to sixty verses and uses fifty-one per cent of the same words in telling the story. It is impossible to hold that Mark is rather an abridgement of Matthew. If such were the case, why should he expand the tale of the healing of the Gadarene demoniac from one hundred and thirty-six words to three hundred and twenty-five when he is unable to find room for the Sermon on the Mount? This conclusion carries with it a further corollary regarding the authorship of our Gospel bearing the name Matthew. Since it is dependent upon the Greek Gospel of Mark, it cannot be attributed to an apostle and publican who knew Jesus well. Though the earlier part of Mark is rearranged, Matthew may well be described as an expanded edition of Mark.

Luke follows the order of Mark almost without change, but he omits one great section (Mark 6. 45–8. 26) entirely. It is futile to speculate why, but we may be sure that Mark is one of "the many" before him to which he refers in his preface. Scholars have debated as to whether the later evangelists used the same edition of Mark that has come down to us or one slightly different. That is as incapable of final settlement as the other question as to whether Mark himself had written sources. However, we are safe in assuming that our Mark was the first attempt systematically to tell the story of Jesus. So important was his work that no one could seek to improve upon it without utilizing this framework.

When the remaining sections of Luke and Matthew are examined, it is discovered that they have a body of material in common. Some of it is identical, word for word, as Luke 11. 24-26 and Matthew 12. 43-45. In other sections, such as the Beatitudes and the Lord's Prayer, there is considerable difference in language. In some cases, such as the parable of the rejected wedding invitation in Matthew 22 and Luke 14, there is hardly more than a common subject. The most plausible explanation is the use of a common source, which is customarily referred to as "Q," from the initial of the German word, *Quelle*, or "source." Countless reconstructions of this hypothetical document have been made. It is sometimes referred to as the "Sayings," because in most of these reconstructions there is a minimum of narrative material. It is safer to say simply that "Q" represents our faith that there was a document. Papias, a writer of the second century, said that Matthew wrote the Logia in the Hebrew language, and that everyone interpreted them as he could. It is very unlikely that at his time the "Q" conjectured by modern scholars still existed. Papias must have been speaking of our Matthew. But his testimony bears witness to the connection of that apostle with the gospel. A possible explanation is that he compiled this document which was embodied in the more complete Gospel.

Many scholars have postulated a third early source for the Gospel of Luke, in addition to Mark and "Q." Much material that is peculiar to him appears quite homogeneous in character. "L" is the usual designation chosen for such a source. A recent upholder of this theory has expanded the idea. Streeter contended that the earliest edition of Luke was a combination of "Q" and "L." Only later did the author come across Mark and insert sections into his earlier draft. In addition, Streeter believed that he could separate another documentary source in Matthew. The resultant view of the literary origins of the synoptic Gospels is called the "four-source theory" (Mark, "Q," "M," and "L") in contrast to the two-source theory of Mark and "Q."[1] In some quarters this theory has been heralded as the definitive solution of the synoptic problem. We cannot however share this confidence.

In evaluating such theories, two psychological factors should be noted—a widespread assumption and a widespread fear. They are not often expressed, but they nevertheless govern the judgment of scholars. The assumption has been that unless material could be assigned to an early written source, it was not likely to be genuine tradition. The fear was that if Luke or Matthew treated a single collection of the sayings of Jesus in so free a fashion as to give us the widely differing versions of the Beatitudes, we could have little assurance that any recorded saying was just as Jesus gave it. By multiplying the hypothetical documents, Streeter can assume that

[1] *The Four Gospels*, pp. 223ff.

whenever the divergence of the Gospels is considerable, the evangelists are copying from different sources.

THE ORAL TRADITION

With many scholars in America and Germany, however, there is little interest in a further search for documents. At best, thirty long years lie between the words that Jesus scattered as the sower sows his seed and the time when they were first committed to writing. They were spoken in Aramaic, but we read them in Greek. What happened to them during this period of oral transmission? That is the vital question. We are not interested primarily in the evangelists; we are interested in Jesus. Our aim must be to understand him better than did they.

Religious educators who have been drilled in a "problem-project" approach should have little difficulty in understanding some of the conditions under which the gospel material was formulated. The Gospels *may* offer a solution to some of our problems. The material contained therein was certainly preserved with the distinct *objective* of helping solve the problems of those first Christians. It is noteworthy that it is the conduct of the disciples that is under consideration in several of the disputes in the Gospels.[2] The Sabbath, ceremonial washings, and unclean foods presented problems upon which they sought a word from Jesus, and the Gospels helped them to meet these problems in the light of his experience.

A similar motive guiding the transmission of the tradition was furnished by the religious needs of the cult. The early Christians were not ethical philosophers, but

[2] Mark 2. 18, 23; 7. 2, 19.

worshipers, and the divine Christ afforded their approach to God. The first connected story which was formulated was unquestionably that of the Passion. Some of its events had no Christian witnesses, but since Jesus was believed to be the Messiah fulfilling all prophecy, gaps could be filled in from the Old Testament. Such an account was essential to meet the psychological needs of the believers who were united in faith.

A third motivating factor is to be found in the needs of the mission. The significance of the message must be told as well as the bare fact. Explanatory comments of the early preachers are therefore to be found in our Gospels. For instance, it would have been quite superfluous for Jesus to *say* to the bystanders, "That ye may know that the Son of man hath authority on earth to forgive sins. . . ."[3] Anyone present could *see* that. But the early apostles apparently used the incident of the healing of the man sick with the palsy in order to bring out that fact about the Jesus whom they were proclaiming. Forgiveness of sins was in his name.

It becomes clear from such considerations as these that even the earliest sources are documents portraying the life of the early church as well as the life of Jesus. The traditions about Jesus were not preserved by disinterested, objective scholars, but by intense believers. They were certain that wherever two or three were gathered together in his name, he was in their midst. The historical memories were adapted to the changing needs of the church under the guidance of that present spirit. A group of contemporary biblical students attempt to follow the course of this development of the tradition

[3] Mark 2. 10.

by a study of the literary forms in which it was preserved. Some of this work has been arbitrary and highly subjective. Yet, no sincere student can neglect this approach. We must distinguish in principle between the faith of the early Christians and the historical facts upon which it was based. A consideration of literary form gives one criterion which is more definite and objective than mere opinion.

A typical example may be drawn from one of the most important forms—that of the parable. It is the considered opinion of most scholars that Jesus spoke genuine parables, and was at most sparing in his use of allegory. When we come, however, to such a story as that of the ten virgins, it can be understood only as an elaborate allegory. The returning bridegroom is the Christ at the Second Coming. But his coming is delayed—which presented a great difficulty to the early church. The wise virgins are the members of the church who are ready; the foolish ones are the careless church members. The man who turns them out when they come knocking at the door is no bridegroom, but the Messiah-Judge at the last day. At that hour it will be quite impossible for the unprepared to borrow oil. The original story of Jesus has been adapted to meet the needs of the church in 80 A. D., when the love of many was beginning to grow cold, and thus has lost its original parabolic form.

Space does not permit a discussion of the many classifications which have been proposed for the gospel material. Easton's *The Gospel Before the Gospels* gives a good survey of this "form-criticism" from a moderately conservative point of view. It is sufficient for our purpose if we appreciate the fact that the community of believers left its imprint on the formulation of the tradition from the very beginning. That being the case, we cannot be satisfied to trace back divergent expressions of Jesus (such as in the Beatitudes) to specific documents. To assign them to sources originating in different centers does not solve the ultimate problem. Even though we assume that the evangelists could not have treated the words of Jesus so freely as to effect so great changes, somewhere in the transmission of the tradition this has taken place. Preservation of a word in even the earliest documents cannot assure us that the material has escaped the influence of the early church.

Hence our study will not be of documents, but of the isolated sections. Each must be judged by itself and for itself, not from the source to which it is assigned. Though Mark was the earliest evangelist, that does not mean that he was able to give a historical outline. Papias wrote in the second century that Mark did not write in order, and modern scholarship would corroborate that judgment. Papias was probably comparing his order with that in Matthew. We agree to this conclusion, not because we prefer that in John, but because we are compelled to recognize that even the earliest narrator did not know the correct order of events. Mark tells his story following now one group of traditions and now another. If the phrase "Son of man" occurs twice in a group of controversies, contrary to Mark's usage elsewhere, it becomes increasingly probable that the five incidents in Mark 2. 1 – 3. 6 came to him as one group. So little is he master of the whole material that he can include a whole list of doublets to stories told earlier, and send Jesus on trips that a glance at the map will reveal to be

impossible.[4]   The impression of aimless wandering after
Jesus leaves Galilee comes from the assembling of isolated
stories in artificial, topical sequence.   Differences of
opinion must always remain in the judgment of the
individual sections; the kind of evidence and demonstration which a scientist expects is never possible in
historical study.   Subjective evaluations can never be
entirely eliminated.   But when we come to reconstruct in a
later chapter the actual mission of the Jesus of history,
the extent of our uncertainty will appear much less than
an abstract discussion of the sources might indicate.

The Fourth Gospel

The Gospel of John presents a problem by itself.   The
authorship is still being debated, but the number of
scholars who assign it to the son of Zebedee is steadily
decreasing.   It would little serve our purpose to call the
roll of modern opinions concerning the authorship of this
remarkable book.[5]   The vital questions for our consideration are the purpose of the author, and the historical
value of his materials.   Some of the upholders of the
ecclesiastical tradition concerning the identity of the
author make such large concessions regarding the subjective element in the book that it loses even for them most
of its value as a historical record of events in Palestine
between 27-30 A. D.

It tells a story very different from that in the first
three Gospels.   There Jesus comes up to Jerusalem for
the first time at the end of his ministry.   In John there

---

[4] Mark 7. 31.
[5] This has been done by the author in the *Methodist Review*, May-June,
1931, pp. 426-431.

are many trips to feasts and an early ministry in Judæa
before the imprisonment of John the Baptist.[6] The length
of the ministry is extended to more than two years. The
cleansing of the Temple is removed from the crucifixion
by this amount of time;[7] the Last Supper is no longer a
Passover, nor does Jesus die on the first day of the
feast.

But there are other more important differences. John
the Baptist has no independent significance as a prophet
of righteousness. He is only a witness to the Lamb of God
that taketh away the sin of the world.[8] The discovery of
the Messiahship of Jesus does not first occur at Cæsarea
Philippi, but from the beginning his disciples "believe"
on him.[9] It is disclosed even to a Samaritan woman,
who acclaims him as "Saviour of the world."[10] The disputes are no longer over the interpretation of the law
but concern his own person, and his relation to the
Father.[11] The Johannine Christ says not, "I am come,"
but "I am."[12]

The central theme is no longer the kingdom of God and
the repentance necessary for those who would receive it.
In fact, it may almost be said that there are no ethical
demands in the fourth Gospel except the simple injunction to love one another.[13] One is tempted to wonder
if that has anything to do with the universal popularity
of this Gospel. Instead of a summons to repentance, it
affirms that we must be born from above of water and
the Spirit.[14] Eternal life is the central theme, and the

[6] John 3. 22.
[7] John 2. 13.
[8] John 1. 7, 26, 29.
[9] John 1. 41, 45.
[10] John 4. 42.

[11] John 5. 26; 7. 26f.; 8. 18f.; 10. 24.
[12] John 4. 26; 6. 48; 8. 12; 10. 11; 11. 25, etc.
[13] John 13. 34.
[14] John 3. 5.

key words are light, life, truth, believe, and witness. A passing reference is made to the older eschatology which looked forward to the coming of the Son of man on the clouds of heaven for the final Judgment.[15] In the experience of the author, however, the new life is already a present possession, and, contrary to Paul, nothing is needed in the future to complete that salvation. Men are judged as they accept or reject now the revelation in Jesus of the Father.[16] There is no new age to come on earth, but in the Father's house are many mansions, to which Jesus has gone in order to prepare for the translation of the disciples.[17]

No longer does Jesus deal with publicans and sinners, scribes and Pharisees, Sadducees and Herodians. His opponents are the unbelieving "Jews." No longer does Jesus speak in parables, in short sententious wisdom sayings, or prophetic outbursts. Long discourses have taken their place, with occasional allegory and very unusual dialogues. In these the other speaker is simply a foil who misunderstands and asks questions in order that Jesus may further expound his spiritual truths.[18] The Jesus of the fourth Gospel is not baptized by human hands; he does not suffer temptation, but challenges his opponents to convict him of sin.[19] The agony of Gethsemane is out of the question; "for this cause came I unto this hour."[20] The cry, "My God, my God, why hast thou forsaken me?" has fallen from the record to be replaced by the triumphant words, "It is finished."[21]

Despite all the zeal of the harmonizers, both pictures

[15] John 5. 28, 29.
[16] John 3. 18.
[17] John 14. 2.
[18] John 3. 4; 4. 11.

[19] John 8. 46.
[20] John 12. 27.
[21] John 19. 30.

cannot be historical.   If we are convinced by the evidence
that one of the original disciples wrote the fourth Gospel,
it can result only in discrediting the historical value of
Mark.   If, on the other hand, it be granted that this
evangelist has rewritten the tradition from the standpoint of the post-Pauline experience of the church, it is of
minor significance who that author was.   In any case,
he was one of the greatest spiritual geniuses of all time.
To call him John, the elder, does not add to our information nor can it detract from the value of a single sentence
to leave him an anonymous disciple of the John of Asia
Minor.

Contemporary scholarship cannot agree with the radical critics of the nineteenth century, however, that the
book is a romance of the second century, utterly without
historical value.   On the contrary, the Jewish character
of the book is more and more emphasized and there is a
growing tendency to fly in the face of tradition and
locate its origin in north Syria.   Certainly, John is to be
preferred at some places to the synoptics.   True, he drew
much of his material from Mark, especially in chapter six,
where his secondary character appears.   Probably he also
knew Luke.   Yet he had some additional tradition from
another source which is not deprived of all historical
worth by the allegorical significance which the author
finds in it.   In fact, the fourth Gospel is probably the
culmination of a growing body of separate tradition, for its
contradictions and disarrangements betray more than one
hand.   On the whole, however, a historical life of Jesus
must be based upon the synoptic Gospels.   John is
primarily an interpreter, not of what the eye saw, or the
ear heard, but what entered into the heart of man.

It must never be supposed that the historian throws into the wastebasket the material which he judges to be secondary. A diamond is a diamond no matter who cuts it. A story about Jesus may have legendary features, but even the unhistorical elements bear testimony to the impression which he made. All of the gospel material stands under the influence of Jesus. A word which reveals that influence may be of much more value to us than many of the words which he actually uttered. The historian is like a coin collector who must know the imprint, and locates its date. The religious worker is satisfied to know if it is gold. But when the religious worker presents Jesus, he is presenting a particular historical character. All our gold does not come from this most precious vein. We honor Jesus most highly when we seek to utilize all the instruments of historical science to set him forth in his true individuality and uniqueness.

SUMMARY

We may bring together, then, the main conclusions of the chapter. (1) The recovery of the authentic Jesus can be made only through a critical sifting of the records. (2) A historical life of Jesus must be based primarily upon the first three Gospels. (3) Even these sources of information are not without interpretative and legendary elements, for they were not written with a merely historical purpose in view. (4) Because the traditions are of varying worth we cannot follow any one Gospel indiscriminately, even the earliest, but must follow what has been sometimes called a "synoptic eclecticism." (5) In the sifting of the tradition, much that the historian rejects as "secondary" remains of great value for the religious educator so long as in his use he does not give a false view of history. We turn, then, to a conscientious effort to discover from our records just who Jesus was, and what he tried to do.

CHAPTER III

THE HISTORICAL PORTRAIT OF JESUS

JESUS was a Jew. He was reared in a devout Hebrew family; his only formal education was in the sacred literature of his people. He thought in the molds and patterns of first-century Judaism. Thus he was able to epitomize in himself and his teaching the best in the religion of the Old Testament. When we consider the significance of Jesus for our age, there is little point in entering into fruitless discussion concerning what he brought that was new. New religious insights are not born out of a clear sky, but are carved out of the rougher marble of our heritage. It is through Jesus that the best in the Old Testament is transmitted to us in living personality.

Our earliest Christian documents, however, present Jesus not as a wise Jewish rabbi of beautiful character, but as the central figure in a cult. Though prayer is more often addressed through him to God than directly to Jesus, he stands on the divine rather than the human side. Yet his followers did not look upon themselves as simply one cult among many. They were the congregation of God; they were the true remnant of Israel; they were the heirs of the promises, the goal and culmination of all history, even now possessing the first fruits of the promised redemption. Who, then, was this Jesus?

We have seen that our sources do not permit us to follow the course of his life. The Gospels were not

designed to satisfy the curiosity of readers concerning
his life development. They give the good news of God.
That opens with the preaching of John the Baptist. A
prophetic voice was heard in the desert regions near the
Jordan. It called men to repentance in the face of the
approaching Judgment. Not national, but ethical qualifi-
cations would avail at that hour. Those who brought
forth fruits worthy of repentance were baptized in the
river. It was not a cult-washing to be repeated frequently, but an eschatological sacrament setting aside
those who were waiting for the "coming one." He would
baptize with the fire that purifies and effects the world
renewal at the Judgment.

It is difficult for us to appreciate the full significance of
John's work, however, for the gospel accounts are seen
through later Christian eyes, where it was taken for
granted that Jesus was the "coming one." There is no
denying that Jesus came with other devout pilgrims to
the baptism of John. To the early Christians, who took
over this rite, the baptism of their Lord (which is already
embarrassing to Matthew) signified the time of the descent
of the Spirit. Such was the interpretation of baptism
when the Gospels were written. Certainly, for Jesus it
meant a committal of life to the will of God. That such
a solemn act must have been accompanied by a new experience of the nearness of God is highly probable. That it
evoked deep searching as to his own task in fulfillment of
the will of God is likewise probable. But all of our
psychologizing must remain tentative and speculative.

In any case, Jesus did not begin his ministry immediately after his baptism. How long he remained with
John the Baptist we do not know, but our earliest source

dates his independent work by the imprisonment of the
Baptist. Jesus did not merely continue the labors of
his great predecessor, to whom he later paid the highest
tribute. He did not himself baptize. He sought the
populous villages of Galilee, rather than the desert
country. He did not follow ascetic practices, but was
often found at banquet tables. His ministry was more
balanced and stood in relation to all of the great religious
heritage of his people. It is against the background of
Judaism that the preaching of Jesus may best be studied.

THE AUTHORITY OF THE TORAH

The Torah embodied for every devout Jew the will of
God. It comprised the first five books of the Old Testament. Much oral preceptive teaching was likewise included under Torah, or teaching. It was for Jesus the
final authority. Its commandments contained the answer
to the quest for eternal life. In such details as the wear-
ing of the tassels customary among the pious, Jesus followed its direction, for we read that a suppliant woman
touched the "hem" of his garment. In no sense did he
reject the sacrificial system prescribed in the law.

At the time of Jesus, Torah included not only the
written Pentateuch, but also the unwritten traditions of
the elders. A static, perfect code could only be a guide to
a living community as it was reinterpreted in growing
tradition. There were many points of difference between
Pharisees and Sadducees regarding the exposition of the
law. Though there are harsh words of Jesus against the
tradition of the elders, we must not suppose that he drew
a line between these and the Old Testament. "The
distinction which Jesus drew was not between oral and

39

written Torah, but between precepts in both which his
prophetic consciousness affirmed as the primary will of
God and others of a secondary or contradictory nature."[1]

Jesus has often been presented as an opponent of the
law. In the eyes of his contemporaries he desecrated the
Sabbath; he ignored many ritual requirements in his
contacts with the godless; he even condemned all divorce,
though it was specifically permitted in the Old Testament.
Luke has set forth the contradiction in the baldest way by
placing the word about divorce immediately following one
affirming the eternity of the law.

But the final appeal of Jesus was always to the will of
God. Though he might violate the ruling interpretations
of the commandment forbidding all work on the Sabbath
day, he appealed to the divine purpose in instituting the
Sabbath—in other words, to the essence of the divine law.
In attacking divorce Jesus did not intend to attack the
law. He appealed to the original purpose of God in
creation as set forth in Genesis. While Mark 7. 15
would cancel whole chapters of Leviticus at one stroke,
his first followers drew no such conclusion, nor is it
probable that Jesus intended more than to emphasize the
primary will of God. In other words, the question at
issue between Jesus and his opponents was not the
authority of the law, but the interpretation of the law.

What principle determined Jesus' insight into the will
of God? We must recognize that in the distilling of
principles from the concrete facts of tradition we are
inevitably influenced by our own evaluations. Our
generation, profoundly humanistic in spirit, is almost
unanimous in finding that principle in reverence for the

---

[1] Branscomb, Harvey, *Jesus and the Law of Moses*, p. 173.

sacredness of personality. It seems to furnish the key in each instance. The welfare of human personality was of greater importance in the sight of God than any day. Human need was sufficient justification for violation of the current interpretation of the Sabbath law. This principle must forbid the heartless turning away from the wife of one's flesh. In such a case it led him to the utmost strictness instead of tolerant liberality. Friendly associations should be maintained with even publicans and sinners, for they too were children of God. As the sick, not the well, need a physician, so the spiritually sick should be sought, not ostracized, by the righteous. So great was the impression of release to the Galilæan peasantry in contrast to the minute casuistry of the schoolmen that the word of Wisdom seemed to speak through him. "Come unto me, all ye that labor and are heavy laden, and I will give you rest. Take my yoke upon you and learn of me." Such was the appeal that came to publicans and sinners.

Since the worth of every personality was assumed as fundamental in an interpretation of the law of God, not merely overt acts of inhumanity were displeasing to him, but also the murderous intent, the lustful thought, and the revengeful spirit. There are abundant parallels from later rabbis to this deepening of the letter of the law. It is unlikely that Jesus was uttering unheard-of novelties in the words which Matthew presents with the implication that Jesus was the new Lawgiver, greater than Moses. The Pharisees themselves used similar formulas in contrasting one portion of the law against another. What they could not admit was his personal assumption of the authority of the individual, prophetic conscience. He struck at the root of the authority of Halakah when he ignored any rabbinical consensus and simply affirmed, "I say unto you." It is probably true that Jesus did not know all of the refinements of the rabbis. He had not studied in their schools; he was, rather, of the untutored "people of the land" designated '*am ha-ares*. Whether he ignorantly misrepresented them on occasion[2] or whether the later authoritative position of the Jews came to that held by Jesus, we shall probably never know with certainty. But no matter how many were the agreements in detail between Jesus and the rabbis, they did not agree upon the principle of interpretation. The Pauline doctrine of the freedom of the spirit could find its roots only in Jesus—a prophetic conscience which interpreted the letter in terms of his own individual insight into the will of God.

While Jesus did not directly affirm a theoretical moral autonomy, he struck at the root of any heteronomy in his summary of the law. Love to God and love to men, not excluding even our enemies, were the great commandments. What love called for he did not presume to dictate. Neither did he discuss whether genuine love could be commanded. We are told to do it, and Paul was only carrying out the implications of Jesus when he affirmed that love was the fulfillment of the law.

THE EARNEST FATHER OF FORGIVING LOVE

Who was the God whose law Jesus sought to interpret? He was not a strange God to men and women whose religion had been nourished in the Old Testament. He was "the God of Abraham, and of Isaac, and of Jacob."

[2] Mark 7. 11.

The God of Jesus was not conceived in philosophical or theological terms. His existence was assumed without argument. There was no occasion to stress his unity, nor his power, nor his righteousness. They were axiomatic for every Jew. God was not conceived in terms of substance with which the worshiper was to come into mystical union. God was essentially moral will. He acted through the normal course of events in making the sun to rise on the evil and the good, and also in the marvelous and miraculous. Hence the symbols were hyperpersonal, even anthropomorphic. The God of Jesus was the earnest Father of forgiving love.

Because of the prominence of the name "Father" in Matthew and John extravagant claims have sometimes been made for Jesus' originality. The family symbol, however, is one of the oldest among religions. It may signify either absolute power or deep obligation. For Jesus it meant God's loving care, which he naïvely illustrated from nature, and even more forcefully from human nature. Not that God's providence excluded human suffering. Physical suffering was under God's control, but he did permit it. No attempt was made to give a reasoned theodicy, nor was there any suggestion that suffering compromises the goodness of God. The divine path called for self-sacrifice, and Jesus took the cup of his own bitter sorrow from the hand of the Father himself. If we feel that some of the words of Jesus contain unjustified optimism, there are others which are marked by resignation. For the child of God anxious care must be supplanted by trust. Faith could work miracles, because it was faith in God, with whom all things were possible. "If ye had faith as a grain of mustard seed, ye would say unto this sycamine tree, Be thou rooted up, and be thou planted in the sea; and it would obey you."

Central in the message of Jesus was the forgiving grace, the seeking love of God. The divine forgiveness knew no bounds and recognized no obstacle but man's own unrepentant heart as revealed in an unforgiving attitude toward his brother. There was joy in heaven over one sinner that repented. Men believed in such a God when Jesus walked among them, for he himself spoke words of forgiveness. There was nothing that man could do to merit the favor of God. It was a gift at his hand, not a wage they had earned. After they had done all, they were yet unrighteous servants. As little children they must receive at the hands of the Heavenly Father. There is nothing to indicate that the poor, the mourners and the sinners who were promised the Kingdom had, as a matter of fact, attained unto the lofty ideal set forth in the Sermon on the Mount. They were the recipients of divine grace. "Fear not, little flock; for it is your Father's good pleasure to give you the kingdom."

We must not suppose, however, that fatherhood was the only symbol used by Jesus. We likewise have master and servant, and king and subject. He did not say that no man could be a son to two fathers, but a slave to two masters. God was for Jesus the Most High, the Lord. "From his mouth the word quivers through us with a suggestion of the limitless, the majestic, the everlasting, the eternal; He rules in holiness and righteousness, who alone is good, a Judge and Destroyer of the evil. He who blasphemes him, commits the greatest sin."[3] He

---

[3] Deissmann, A., *The Religion of Jesus and the Faith of Paul*, pp. 90-91.

taught his disciples to pray in lowly humility, "Hallowed be thy name." No sickly sentimentality characterized the relation of God to his children. That needs emphasis in an age which has exchanged the thought of "sinners in the hands of an angry God" for spoiled children in the arms of an indulgent grandmother.

But we must go farther. We have called the God of Jesus the earnest Father. He had moral objectives in history. All human roads did not lead unto the way everlasting for He was dead in earnest. Many modern men deduce from the Fatherhood of God a universalism that will of necessity make everything right for all. Such was not the logic of Jesus. Men faced the Judgment. Divine grace did not mean moral indifference on the part of God. A crisis was at hand. An emergency faced all men. "Be not afraid of them that kill the body, and after that have no more that they can do. . . . Fear him, who after he hath killed hath power to cast into hell; yea, I say unto you, Fear him."

THE COMING KINGDOM OF GOD

What was the nature of this crisis which lent impelling motivation to every word which Jesus spoke? It is to be found in the call with which he is reported to have opened his ministry. "Repent, for the kingdom of God is at hand." The long-awaited dream of his people was about to come to pass. The sovereignty of God, till then confined to those who in loving obedience took upon themselves the yoke of the kingdom, was about to be realized in outward, visible expression. The end of the age and the coming of the Messianic era were upon them.

This kingdom was not to be established by force.

45

Rather than resist a Roman soldier in throwing off the hated yoke, they should go with him two miles. Nothing that man could do could usher in the Kingdom. Jesus did not say, as did certain later rabbis, that if Israel would only keep one Sabbath, the Kingdom must come. It was not a social order that man could build. All that man could do was to get ready for the new society that God would send. The disciples were sent out two by two on a hurried mission of preparedness. So great was the urgency that they should not tarry in any place, nor burden themselves with anything beyond the most meager essentials. The coming of this kingdom could not be calculated by outward signs, but suddenly it would be in their midst. As there was no warning in the days of Noah, so now. As Jonah's preaching was the only sign for the people of Nineveh, so his call to repentance was the only sign for this generation. There were those standing there who would not taste of death till they saw the Kingdom coming with power.

So imminent, in fact, was this new age that its powers were already manifest in his own ministry. If the demons were subject unto him, it was a sign that the Kingdom had come upon them. In jubilation he greeted the return of his disciples, "I beheld Satan fallen as lightning from heaven." When emissaries from John the Baptist inquired if he were the "coming one," Jesus simply pointed to the works that were being done. "The blind receive their sight and the lame walk . . . and the poor have good tidings preached to them." These were, of course, but small beginnings. But the kingdom of heaven was like unto a mustard seed; from the smallest seed would come a great tree. So likewise these small beginnings were but a dim foretaste of the new age which God would send. The day to which prophets and kings looked forward was about to dawn.

This was a cause of rejoicing for some. Blessed were the poor, the humble, and the persecuted, not because deprivation is a blessing, but because the Kingdom would be for them. Unto others his message resounded forth as a prophetic woe. Woe unto the rich, the insincere religious stage actors, and to the Galilæan cities that turned a deaf ear to his call for repentance. "It shall be more tolerable for Tyre and Sidon in the day of judgment than for you." So great was the coming good that it was worth any price it might cost. An out-and-out decision must be made. They must count the cost even though it meant estrangement from family and loved ones. Do not turn back, but resolutely pay it.

The expectation of such an impending catastrophe could not but leave its mark upon the ethics of Jesus. The term "interim-ethic" has frequently been used, but not always with a clear understanding of what is involved. It may refer to special requirements because of the urgency of the moment. Some of the words of Jesus to those who were to "follow" him in a literal and not merely a metaphorical sense are obviously such. They must sever all family ties, abandon their property, and fully expect to meet persecution. Necessarily such demands did not rest upon all who earnestly awaited the coming Kingdom. In the second place, an interim-ethic may refer to temporary requirements that will cease when the Kingdom comes. Unquestionably, there are these in Jesus, but it does not follow that the teaching is thereby invalidated for men who do not recognize the presence of the same crisis. For example, the word previously cited on divorce is obviously interim-ethic, for if there is neither marriage nor giving in marriage in the resurrection, questions surrounding divorce have no applicability in the coming age.

But this illustration suggests a third significance of interim-ethic—eternal standards without relation to time. In the dawning light of an eternal world Jesus did not think in terms of "practical" adjustments to grim reality. What was the unconditional will of God which a man should resolutely accept in the face of the immediate emergence of eternity in the midst of time? A love that knew no bounds was the only adequate principle. If the inwardness of the ethics of Jesus was uninfluenced by his hope, the same can hardly be said for his radicalism. "So little as the demands of Jesus can be deduced in themselves from the expectation of the end, one must the more consider that their radicalism and unconcerned-ness with their possibility and feasibility can only be understood from the standpoint of eschatology."[4] His was a call not merely to repentance, but to the perfection of God himself.

Unless the importance of the Kingdom hope is recognized, we will gravely misjudge Jesus. The prevalence of the language of rewards will appear debasing unless we see the great alternative—participation or nonparticipation in the coming Kingdom. It explains many of his emphases. Humility is always a virtue, but it needed stress for those already dreaming of their place at the right hand of the Messiah. Faithfulness and watchfulness may always be desirable, but their importance in

---

[4] Troeltsch, *Die Soziallehre*, p. 40.

the gospel tradition was due to this particular emergency. It is more significant in explaining the absence of much which we seek to learn from Jesus. He had no occasion to discuss the state, the reorganization of society upon the basis of new motives, the humanization of industry, or any of the other concerns of the so-called social gospel. Since the present age would not survive more than a generation, his whole attention was concentrated upon getting individuals ready. Their cultural development did not concern him in the slightest. These things afforded no preparation for the age to come.

The most crucial issue lies in the relation of Jesus to poverty and wealth. The assumption of all modern humanitarianism is that poverty is a curse which ought to be removed. Jesus considered not poverty but riches a curse, because Mammon was the great competitor of God. It was next to impossible for a rich man to enter the kingdom of God, for riches presented the greatest of all spiritual perils. The abiding truth of this insight does not alter the insufficiency of its guidance for an age that gives a positive evaluation to culture, looking forward to countless generations of possible progress. The question as to the authority of Jesus is raised here in its most difficult form.

Finally, it should be noted that while the Kingdom hope presents a social ideal, and one for all people, it explains the restriction of the ministry of Jesus to his own people. The requirements for admission to the Kingdom were ethical and not national; his illustrations of God's care were taken from nature, not from Jewish history. But whatever contact he had with Gentiles—which was hardly avoidable in "Galilee of the Gentiles" and during

his exile from the realms of Herod Antipas—was not of
his own seeking. Not even among Samaritans did he
make it a point to carry on his work, though he might
use them as an example to shame his fellow countrymen.
It was among Israel that the preparation must be made,
but when the great day dawns, "they shall come from the
east and west, and from the north and south, and shall
sit down in the kingdom of God." Hence Antioch and
Ephesus were not potential fields for ministry. He must
set his face steadfastly to go up to Jerusalem.

The Person of Jesus

It is impossible, however, to isolate the message of
Jesus from the man. He was inseparably identified with
his work. That Person can be considered best under the
same three headings we have just discussed. Jesus was,
of course, a teacher. But this category, so prominent
in our age (though as a rule we do not place teachers upon
the pinnacle, as in China, for instance), must not be over-
stressed. Simply as the wisest of rabbis he would not
have been heard of outside Palestine. His relationship to
his disciples was not that of a teacher to scholars, but of
a saint to his adoring followers. The inspiration of his
personality is the presupposition for the later resurrection
experiences. He gave the impression of that numinous
quality which R. Otto has so stressed in *The Idea of the
Holy*. Mark records, "And Jesus was going before them;
and they were amazed; and they that followed were
afraid." But they followed him to Jerusalem. It was
not a learned professor who there drove the money-
changers out of the Temple. It was a dynamic figure
whose flaming zeal compelled obedience. It was the

words of the Holy One of God which were preserved by the disciples.

If Jesus did not teach a new God, at least we find in him a new realization of divine sonship. This is frankly a faith judgment which cannot be demonstrated by texts. Jesus was too religious a man to go about talking of his own relation to God. We are entirely dependent upon the impression which is recorded by others, and the few words ascribed to him by the community expressive of their own belief about him. Our windows into the prayer life of Jesus may be tiny indeed, but they are wide enough to reveal a trust and a confidence that explain why Paul used as his characteristic formula, "The God and Father of our Lord Jesus Christ." Jesus had revealed God unto them, not because metaphysically divine attributes were perceivable in his person, but because, in his own filial devotion, the God who awakened it was made clearer unto men. We will not believe that he who said, "Everyone that exalteth himself shall be humbled," was accustomed to personal boasting. The unique sonship of Jesus is much less clear from a word such as, "Neither doth any know the Father, save the Son," or, "No one cometh unto the Father, but by me," than from the simple request of the disciples, "Lord, teach us to pray." He was revealing God unto them by the way he lived with God day by day. "Upon the countenance of the praying Jesus rests the clear reflection of the countenance of his God."[5]

But Jesus was conscious of a unique mission from God. "I am come" is a phrase which the tradition continually placed upon his lips. What could his special

[5] Deissmann, A., *op. cit.*, p. 68.

mission from God be? Was it simply to announce the coming age as its last prophet or was he the Anointed of God himself? There can be no doubt that the early church preached Jesus as the Messiah. His own attitude is not so clear.

It should be borne in mind that messiahship has nothing to do with the so-called divinity of Christ. It was an office, not a nature. Furthermore, in many expressions of the messianic hope, there was no place for any king other than Jehovah himself. Many expositors of Jesus have discussed at great length his spiritual interpretation of messiahship. It is contended that he withheld self-disclosure until he had educated the disciples to his own understanding. Apart from the fact that there is not a shred of evidence for it, it may well be asked what point there was in choosing a particular title at the same time that one rejected all its known meanings?

There was, of course, more than one expectation. Probably the most common was that of a Davidic king. That Jesus rejected this there can be no question. The phrase that is upon the lips of Jesus is that of "Son of man," but it presents a most perplexing problem. In Aramaic it could mean only "the man." It is used in the Gospels in three very different senses, namely, as equivalent to the first person, in relation to suffering and the Passion, and with eschatological reference to the figure coming on the clouds of heaven. (Daniel 7. 13.) In which of these meanings did Jesus use the word, if at all? There is little doubt that many of our references are secondary, and to be ascribed to an early stage in the theology of the early church. We believe, however, that some usage goes back to Jesus himself. But did he refer to himself or to another? Was it a recognized name for the heavenly Messiah among the people, considering the paucity of the literary remains which thus use it? Did Jesus publicly proclaim himself in such terms?

It is not certain from our earliest and most authentic sources that he did ever publicly make any messianic claims. The cleansing of the Temple may be considered simply as a prophetic act. Only the fourth Gospel knows of debates with the "Jews" upon the subject, obviously debates of the time of the evangelist himself. Whatever may have been the intention of Jesus and the festival pilgrims accompanying him in the so-called triumphal entry, the people called him a prophet, not a messianic claimant, and the hozannas were for the Kingdom, not the king.[6] But these facts need not cause us to doubt that among the disciples there had arisen the belief that Jesus was the Christ. The confession from Peter at Cæsarea Philippi is conclusive evidence. Jesus' injunction to silence, however, presents a messianic secret which demands explanation. The most probable would be, that the lowly carpenter of Nazareth of course was not now the Anointed of God, except in an anticipatory sense. He was the one appointed of God with whom the Kingdom would come in the future as portrayed in apocalyptic imagery. Such at least is the situation in the account of the hearing before the high priest. The direct affirmation of Jesus concerns only the coming of the Son of man on the clouds of heaven. He does not confess any messianic career in the past.

We are not to think of Jesus as making claims for himself. It was the Kingdom that was central in his

[6] Matthew 21. 10; Mark 11. 10.

preaching and work. But if, in the inscrutable providence of God, he was chosen as God's final representative, must he not pray, "Thy will be done"? The only tenable solution of the messianic problem in the career of Jesus is a religious one. When seen in the light of contemporary ideas, it may appear to be more of a liability than an asset so far as our interest in Jesus is concerned. Many of those who deny that Jesus considered himself in any sense a Messiah mean thereby to honor him. But our only criterion can be the most reasonable implication of the facts. They seem to us to indicate that Jesus did expect to be the coming heavenly "Son of man."

THE FATE OF JESUS

We have endeavored to sketch the substance of the Galilæan preaching of Jesus. Just how soon retirement became prudent it is impossible for us to say. To what extent the opposition of the Pharisees was responsible in addition to the hostility of Herod Antipas, the ruler of Galilee, can never be fully known. Indications of friendly intercourse with the Pharisees are not lacking. It should not be forgotten that they were a religious party with no legal authority. They were not as numerous in Galilee as in Judæa, and some of the disputes which Mark locates in Galilee may well have taken place nearer the capital. Mark is almost certainly in error in confining the Jerusalem ministry to a single week. One of the most certain results of recent synoptic criticism is the realization that Mark's order is not chronological. In Mark 3 the opposition had already come to a head, but it was first at Jerusalem that the tentacles actually closed about Jesus.

We cannot ascribe this Pharisaic opposition to the

early church, but the fact remains that it was not until the chief priests took a hand that Jesus was actually taken into custody. In other words, it was the Sadducaic party that gave the final impetus to do away with him. Their opposition is certainly not due to mere differences of opinion over the resurrection. Some connection with the cleansing of the Temple by Jesus, as in the Oberammergau Passion play, is altogether probable. The monopolistic extortions of the priests were being interfered with by this prophetic representative of the Galilæan peasants. According to Christian tradition, it was one of the intimate disciples who betrayed Jesus. Not a few scholars have rejected this as legendary, but the intriguing possibility cannot be disregarded that what Judas betrayed was the messianic secret. It was not simply the place where they could find Jesus that he told. Judas confirmed their suspicions that this was really a dangerous messianic movement, for Jesus looked upon himself as the Messiah. It was the Sadducaic priestly party that cast the vote against Jesus. Their refusal to accept the new belief in a resurrection accompanied a weakening of vital interest in the hope of their fathers. It is unlikely that the real ground for attacking him was blasphemy, for "Son of God" could only be blasphemy as understood by later hellenistic Christians. Luke has preserved the essence of the charge, "We found this man perverting our nation, and forbidding to give tribute to Cæsar, and saying that he himself is Christ a king." The word concerning the Temple which figured in the trial, probably referred to its abolishment (in the new age to come)? or by Rome?

That Jesus saw the tentacles of opposition closing around him is certain, though the predictions of the

Passion in the Gospels are all colored by the actual events. The daring appeal at Jerusalem was not meeting with success. What was to become of his work? Would not God miraculously intervene to save him? There is no evidence that Jesus believed that in the woes of the last time the righteous were to be preserved from all harm. They were called upon to suffer. Could it be that his death was a necessary prelude to the coming of the Kingdom, and his coming as the heavenly Son of man? For a suffering and dying Messiah there was no precedent. Enticing as is the belief that the fifty-third chapter of Isaiah pointed the way, it cannot be denied that sure traces of this application in the earliest Christian community are not to be found with certainty. But there was abundant precedent in the evaluation of the vicarious suffering and death of the martyrs of the Maccabean Age.

On the eve of the Passover season, as Jesus sat at meat with his disciples as was their custom in common meals, he did an uncommon thing. Parabolic utterances had been characteristic of his popular preaching. But now, as did prophets of old, he arose to act a parable. As the bread was broken and the wine poured out for them, so would his body be broken, and his blood shed. As they drank, he said, "I shall no more drink of the fruit of the vine, until that day when I drink it new in the kingdom of God." His approaching death would in some inscrutable way be a means of bringing the Kingdom to them. One similar word is found in Mark 10. 45. It is probable that it is secondary to Luke 22. 27. It should be noticed, however, that the context of the famous logion is not in relation to the forgiveness of sins. That is not dependent upon the death of Jesus. It was with reference to places in the coming age that Jesus is reported to have said, "The Son of man came . . . to give his life a ransom for many." His death would be for them a gateway of entrance into the Kingdom.

The disciples fled at the capture of Jesus. Only a little group of faithful women witnessed the crucifixion from afar. The precious bits of information were filled in by Old Testament prophecies so that a consecutive story of the Passion might be told for the adoring disciples. It was probably from an eye-witness such as Simon of Cyrene that the last cry was reported—"My God, my God, why hast thou forsaken me!" The experiences of the dying Jesus are impenetrable for our profane eyes. Did he expect a miraculous interposition at the last minute? It is not for us to speculate. It would be blasphemous for our unholy curiosity to seek to lift the veil that envelops his Passion. The historian can only bow in reverence and adoration beside the humblest believer.

THE INTERPRETATION OF JESUS

The life of Jesus should close with the entombment of the body by Joseph of Arimathæa. But it was only the beginning of his influence. A few brief days and the band of Galilæan disciples was once more in Jerusalem, and not in frightened retirement. As they broke bread together awaiting the coming of the Christ, they proclaimed not only that the name of the Messiah would be Jesus. This Jesus had been raised from the dead, for he had appeared unto them.

When we turn from this simple statement to recon-

struct the details, we are met with many difficulties.   The
accounts are full of contradictions.   The earliest Gospel,
Mark, closes with the terrified flight of women from the
tomb, who tell no one of their inability to find the body
of Jesus.   The fundamental truth is not that the disciples
could not find a dead Christ, but that they did find a
living Christ.   The account by Paul was written probably
thirty years earlier than any other which we possess and
records the common apostolic faith.   Peter was the rock
of the apostolic faith whose "turning again" was the real
beginning of the church.[7]   The nature of these experiences
is naturally unfathomable to the historian.   But Paul
knew nothing of a physical ascension which separated the
earlier appearances from his own.   The essence of all
was spiritual experience.

One who has learned from Paul that "flesh and blood
cannot inherit the kingdom of God" will have no interest
in what became of the body that was laid away in the
grave.   Only sense-bound, materialistic minds identify
personality with a particular body of flesh.   But there
were such in the early church.   If the reality of the
experiences of Peter and the others was to be made plain
to them, it must be expressed in such corporeal forms as
eating and bodily contact.   It was a tragedy that the
spiritual view of Paul was not maintained in the second
century and afterward.   For some still a rejection of this
crass, materialistic view of the resurrection, which Paul
definitely repudiated, is tantamount to a denial of the
resurrection itself.

The belief that Jesus had been raised by God from the
dead and elevated to his right hand, because he had

[7] 1 Corinthians 15. 3ff.

appeared unto them, transformed the lives of the disciples. Worship was now directed through Christ. The disciples did not preach primarily the ethical-religious personality of Jesus, but what God had done and would do through him. Historical Christianity was from the first *about* the Christ whom God had raised from the dead.

As we survey the writings preserved by the Gentile churches which developed from the original Jewish communities, we are impressed with the variety of the figures drawn upon to express what Jesus meant to them. We may attempt a rough threefold classification which does not avoid overlapping, but which suggests the sources of the titles applied to Jesus. There are metaphors drawn from everyday life. Jesus is called the door, the true vine, the light, our captain, and apostle. Other figures were suggested by the Old Testament, such as the Good Shepherd, and the Servant of the Lord. Others which are found in the Old Testament were likewise suggested by a comparison with other religions. Such were High Priest, and Mediator (confined to Hebrews), and especially Lord, commonest in Paul. While Saviour is found in the Septuagint, the Greek translation of the Old Testament, it is definitely a Gentile title.

This bewildering array of names (which might be further extended) offers no explanation of the personality of Jesus. They merely suggest comparisons which expressed his meaning to the first believers. Already in the first century we find the rejection of interpretations which seemed false. It could not be accepted that Jesus was only one among many angelic beings, nor that Christ did not really suffer in the flesh. A uniform, reasoned interpretation of Jesus we do not find.

Two types of attempts may be distinguished. The first (and earliest) looked upon Jesus as a man, adopted into the divine world. We can trace through the New Testament the progressive pushing back of the date of this adoption. The term "Son of God," which could only have a theocratic significance in Judaism, was taken literally among the Gentile converts. At first Jesus was considered the Son of God at the resurrection. The transfiguration and the baptism stories, as they stand, represent successive stages in pushing the divine Sonship back into the lifetime of Jesus. This process of reinterpretation comes to its climax in the birth-stories of Matthew and Luke, where it is affirmed that Jesus was "Son of God" because the Holy Spirit replaced a human father.

Such an interpretation, however, did not satisfy many of the thinkers of New Testament times. For Paul, the author of Hebrews, and John, Christ was a pre-existent being. John alone uses the term "logos," but the idea of a mediator of creation is already to be found in the earlier writers. Paul and Hebrews still definitely subordinate Jesus unto God, but in John, the final affirmation of faith concerning Jesus is "My Lord and my God." But how this eternal, pre-existent logos, sharing in divine omnipotence and omniscience, was to be related to the human consciousness of a man is not solved. In the fourth Gospel the story of Jesus is rewritten in terms of the logos-Christ of faith.

We of the twentieth century turn back to the Jesus of history who inspired these tributes and all of this speculation. We must begin not with old interpretations, but with Jesus himself. As Peter discovered that he was more than Moses or the greatest of the prophets, so we must personally discover his meaning in relation to our own categories. We have the same right that the first Christians possessed to express the meaning of Jesus out of the terms of our own experience. As we follow him, as we face his compelling alternatives, we shall discover who he is.

But we cannot begin our thought of Jesus in modern terms. We see him most vividly as prophet and teacher speaking out of the soul of his time and people. A universalized portrait is pale and lifeless. A modern Jesus is an anachronism or at best a creation of pious imagination. We must see once again the earnest Galilæan who did not believe that religion was the concern alone of the professional priest and scribe. It was a question of life itself for every sincere man. He came out of the obscurity of silent years to touch the life of what would be called "a backward province" for a few brief months. Superficially viewed, it was a very insignificant event in human history. Only when it is viewed in relationship with the whole religious development of his people with their messianic beliefs and hopes can that life be seen in any adequate perspective. But when we see him as he truly was, our age, as those which have gone before it, feels called upon to turn to the highest categories we know to express, and then imperfectly, what he means to us.

CHAPTER IV

SOME PROBLEMS IN THE LIFE OF JESUS

ONE of the most difficult of the problems surrounding the teaching of the life of Jesus is to be found in the miracles which so profusely adorn the pages of the Gospels. They were written in an age when belief in miracle was universal. It would argue against the authenticity of these books if they contained no miracle stories, for God was looked upon as a God of power who revealed himself in the marvelous. Throughout the centuries miracle has been the best-loved child of faith. But our generation is becoming increasingly influenced by the scientific view of the world. Science cannot admit miracle, for she cannot confess that her task of understanding is doomed to failure at the outset. Science assumes the rationality of the universe. While the unknown and mysterious remain extensive, she has no place for supernatural events not subject to investigation.

Obscurity will surround any discussion of miracle until we define our terms. Most upholders of the miraculous to-day will insist that they do not mean the contravention of natural law. They sometimes define a miracle as an event of significance for religion. For our purpose, we mean by "miracle" the marvelous events recorded in the Gospels. Did they happen or not? What use will the Bible teacher make of such material? We may leave to the philosophers the further refinement of definitions and the elaboration of a world-view.

It is important, however, to see clearly that in this sphere of ultimate interpretation much is at stake. We are vitally concerned in a religious view of the universe. We should appreciate the protest of religious philosophers against an exclusively mechanistic view of the world. If there were no other aspect than this in which to view it, religion would be meaningless. We do crave support for the belief that there are creative energies at work, and that God is not a helpless victim of impersonal laws. But wherein lies the greatest value for religion? Is not the dependable world of order which is the postulate of science of greater significance, pointing as it does to a God who is faithful? Increasing numbers believe that dependence upon the capricious chance of occasional miracle cannot be compared to adjustment to a dependable universe as a ground for faith.

In our approach to this problem we must never lose sight of the practical result in the life of the pupil. Small children, at least, who have been brought up on fairy-story books, will not be troubled at first by miracle stories in the Bible. But if we use them to teach such lessons as the loving care of God, what deduction will a child draw? Will he expect to find the evidence for God's care in such marvelous incidents in his own life? If they do not materialize, what will be the conclusion he will draw as to the existence of such a God of loving care? Why should God have confined his help to Bible times if he loves us truly? Do the defenders of gospel miracles believe that they are exalting Jesus, or do they want to believe in some providential interposition in their own lives now?

Analysis of the miracle stories shows that they do not

all stand upon the same level. Many of the stories of healings are to be understood in the light of the long history of faith-healing.[1] They may be unusual events, but they stand on the plane of observable and repeatable happenings. Because of inexact diagnosis, from our point of view, it is impossible to judge conclusively concerning such incidents as demon exorcisms. Some, however, are quite beyond any verifiable analogies in the history of mental healing. The records of antiquity, however, are full of such stories.[2] The Roman Catholic Church makes it a condition for the canonization of a saint that he must have performed three accredited miracles. Most of them are miracles of healing. Protestants usually reject these extra-canonical and ecclesiastical miracles. But, then, it should be asked, By what right do we draw a line about Scripture and refuse the same scientific criticism to the events reported there? We are accustomed to look upon the healing stories as demonstrations of the compassion of Jesus, but in our sources they are revelations of his power as much as the so-called nature miracles.

What may be said concerning a *literal* interpretation of the miracles? Just this, that if they are true—if a man can sometimes walk on water, or multiply loaves of bread at will—the law-abiding universe of science does not exist. It is fruitless to take refuge in the assumption that Jesus utilized other laws which are unknown to us. Nowhere in the New Testament is Jesus assigned superior scientific insight. We believe that he was unique, but that uniqueness did not lie in an anticipation of scientific discoveries which are still to come. Nor do we obtain a

[1] Micklem, E. R., *Miracles and the New Psychology.*
[2] Case, S. J., *Experience With the Supernatural in Early Christian Times.*

loophole for such events by appealing to the "new physics." There may be a principle of indeterminism in the very structure of the atom, but that does not make one whit more credible the immediate changing of molecules of water into molecules of wine. Our Gospels intend to relate miracles of omnipotent power. To assign to Jesus scientific knowledge on the basis of no evidence but our desire to rationalize the miracle can only end in denying that he was "very man of very man."

Nor do we gain anything by pointing to the greater marvels of our own day. To the mind untrained in electricity and wave phenomena it is more marvelous to sit by our fireside and listen to words spoken on the other side of the earth than anything we can read in the New Testament. But there is an absolute difference. This achievement is due to the gradual building up of experimental knowledge so that some men at least understand the processes. Once understood, it always can be accomplished whenever the conditions are met. Furthermore, the achievements of radio do not point out the divinity of its discoverers, nor are they in any special sense acts of God. These marvels are triumphs of scientific inquiry. If a parallel with biblical miracles be drawn, the same secular significance of them must be accepted.

This leads us to a further objection to the literal interpretation of the miracles. It centers the uniqueness of Jesus not in character but in nonmoral power. It makes him not a Saviour but a magician. The primitive mind is impressed by mysterious power. The educated conscience bows down only before character and worth. As a matter of fact, miracles do not afford the basis for unique claims. Elisha and Elijah are also said to have raised the dead to life again.[3] If it were true, it would not make either one the Son of God. When Jesus was asked to legitimate his work by a sign from heaven his reply was, "Why doth this generation seek a sign? verily I say unto you, There shall no sign be given."[4] An ethical appeal for moral and religious ends has no connection with outward signs of power. If Jesus reveals an ethical God, that revelation will not lie in physical marvels, but in the moral and spiritual transformation of life. "The personality of Christ leads to a God who is first, foremost, and always ethical; the traditional miracle concept leads to a God who is arbitrary, if not, indeed, unmoral. The God revealed by Christ has little or nothing in common with the God suggested by the notion that laws are violated for the advantage of some and not of others."[5]

As a matter of fact, the miracles are customarily used in an allegorical way, even by those who most strenuously contend for their historicity. The Jesus whom they preach is one who opens the eyes of the spiritually blind, heals the leprosy of sin, and speaks a word of calm to the troubled hearts of men. They expect to continue the healing ministry of Jesus in quite law-abiding ways. Why, then, should we have difficulty in accepting the belief that this explains how *some* of the stories arose? Is it accidental that just before Mark takes Jesus onto Gentile soil he has him unstop the ears of a deaf man, and open the eyes of a blind man?[6] Was that not what was happening in the name of the risen Christ on Gentile

[3] 1 Kings 17. 22; 2 Kings 4. 35.
[4] Mark 8. 12.
[5] Wright, C. J., *Miracle in History and Modern Thought*, p. 374.
[6] Mark 7. 31ff.; 8. 22ff.

soil at the time he was writing? As a matter of fact, for John, the miracles, or signs, as he calls them, are texts for sermons. The feeding of the five thousand becomes the basis for a Eucharistic discourse upon Jesus, the bread of life.[7] Instead of invoking some unknown power contravening all we know about the physical universe, might we not suspect that the original incident had something to do with the breaking of bread with Jesus by a crowd in anticipation of the messianic banquet?

It is not difficult to allegorize some of the miracle stories so that they may be the vehicles of helpful lessons. We may, for instance, show what happened when a little boy brought "all" to Jesus. We may contrast Jesus asleep in a vessel amidst the storm, confident that he was in the hands of God, with Jonah, asleep in the hold because he thought he had successfully run away from God. Incidental aspects of other incidents may be drawn upon, such as the co-operation of the four friends in helping one sick of the palsy into the presence of Jesus. The peril to be avoided is that we cast a veil of vagueness over the question as to whether these occurrences actually happened as definite events in time.

There should be no hesitancy in admitting legendary incidents where they are to be found. It is utterly false to insist in such a case that the whole portrait of Jesus is evaporated into legend. In practical life no one refuses to believe the testimony of his senses just because they occasionally deceive him. As we have seen from our discussion of the sources, each incident and saying must be judged by itself. One doubtful incident does not throw suspicion upon another. If we are to love God with

7 John 6. 53ff.

our minds, we must begin in the discriminating use of the Book which records the story of the progressive discovery of his will.

Far more important than to defend the biblical miracles is it to help our students understand the relation of God to the world, and the way that he now works in human lives. To encourage one to look for God in the gaps or breaks in the causal nexus is to do him a disservice and hamper his religious development. A God whom we can understand must be a principle operating in the whole process of life, not in a few special acts which we designate miracles and around which we set up, against science, a sign, "No trespassing!" We must not make the mistake of assuming that nothing that is impossible for us was possible for an extraordinary personality like Jesus. We must insist, rather, that what appeared then as marvelous is no more a demonstration of divinity than the laying of his hands upon little children to bless them. We have no reason to suppose that any event in his life could not be understood by scientific investigation in the same measure that happenings now can be so understood. After the scientist has investigated all processes, and posited no gaps for supernatural interference, nothing is fully explained. The division between a religious and an unreligious view of the world is in the philosophic interpretation of the *whole*, not in a division between natural and supernatural events.

What attitude, therefore, is the conscientious religious teacher to follow in regard to the gospel miracles? If our aim is to convey truth as well as to have a "feeling of honesty," the course we will pursue must naturally vary with the degree of maturity of the students. If miracles are not of value to us, we will not choose to use them unnecessarily. But it will be a part of our task as religious educators to see that students come to a constructive solution of the problem. They must come to see the distinction between the historical evidence for an event and the religious interpretation of that event (miracle). The evangelists who believed that nothing was impossible report some events which are incredible to us. We should frankly say, for instance, that the story of Jesus walking on the water was told by disciples who thought it was evidence of his divine power. We do not know just how the story arose. It is an illustration of their faith in him, not proof upon which to base our faith. We will believe in his leadership upon other grounds. While we are not warranted in saying that this event *could* not have happened, we should affirm that there is not sufficient evidence that it *did* happen. If it did happen, it would be for us no warrant for his religious and ethical leadership, but a mysterious physical event as yet unexplained. It would remain a problem for scientific research along with "cosmic rays" and a cure for cancer. The religious man who has experience of a God of ethical love in Jesus has no greater interest in one than the other.

THE USE OF LEGEND

The problem of the use of legend is akin to that of miracle in that it likewise concerns material which arouses our skepticism. We have chosen to treat first of all a story which might more accurately be deemed a miracle— the virgin birth or supernatural generation of Jesus. We believe, however, that it is an integral part of the "birth legends" and hence comes more fittingly here.

This problem is unique because the Christmas stories are universally used for pupils of all ages and are unquestionably among the most precious remains of the early church. In this case neglect is indefensible. But how are they to be used—as historical and doctrinal truths, or as poetic interpretations of the significance of the birth of Him who was looked upon by the gospel writers as the divine Son of God? With small children the virgin birth may be ignored, but not with maturer students who are faced at once by the problem, must the supernatural generation be accepted as a fact?

All that has been said regarding the "miraculous" in the last section applies to the subject of the virgin birth. All of the arguments advanced against seeking God in the "gaps" must be considered in this connection as well. We may therefore confine ourselves to the historical evidence for the "event."

It should be recognized that there are two traditions in the New Testament concerning the parentage of Jesus, not one. The belief in the fatherless generation is found in only two passages, neither of which is part of an early document.[8] Elsewhere the belief is expressed that Jesus was a descendant of David. This is witnessed not only in the genealogies but in other places in the New Testament.[9] It may readily be granted that incidental references to Joseph as the father of Jesus may mean nothing more than legal parentage.[10] But when emphasis is laid in gospel narratives upon the fulfillment of prophecy in the descent of Jesus from the Davidic line, it would hardly be

---

[8] Matthew 1. 18; Luke 1. 35.
[9] Mark 10. 47; Romans 1. 3; 2 Timothy 2. 8; Revelation 5. 5.
[10] John 1. 45; 6. 42.

a sufficient basis that he was *adopted* into that line. The genealogies are of Joseph and not Mary.[11] At least one of them must be unhistorical, for two different genealogies cannot both be true. But the significant fact for our attention is that the persons who compiled and preserved them must have believed that Jesus was the son of David, and through Joseph rather than Mary. This tradition may conceivably be wrong, but at least it is a different tradition from that of the virgin birth.

The historian can naturally have nothing to say concerning the truth or falsity of the virgin birth. The claim rests ultimately upon the testimony of one witness— Mary herself. Our only criterion can be whether during the ministry of Jesus she manifested the kind of attitude toward him that would be expected of a mother to whom such an unusual experience had come. What would be "expected" is, of course, a subjective criterion. But the historian cannot fail to point out that none of the earlier Gospels knows anything about a tradition which placed her at the foot of the cross at the hour of crucifixion. Not one simile based on human motherhood falls from the lips of Jesus. We only read that his mother and brethren came to take him home, because they thought he was "beside himself."[12]

Many express the belief that it was eminently "fit" that such a unique person should come into the world in this unique way. But if a human father was inappropriate, why was not a human mother likewise a contaminating connection with sinful humanity? The exaltation of virginity which is implied in a stress upon the "fitness"

---

[11] Matthew 1. 1ff.; Luke 3. 23ff.
[12] Mark 3. 21, 31.

of the fatherless generation is hardly an ideal to appeal to the youth of our age.

We have not made the event one whit more credible to the modern mind by demonstrating—at least to our own satisfaction—that the beautiful gospel stories could not have been derived from either pagan or Jewish sources. It is not surprising that the genealogy of legends cannot be traced at this distance. We will recognize that the stories represent one step in the explanation by early Christians as to how Jesus was Son of God. We believe that no merely physical explanation is of the slightest importance in interpreting a moral and spiritual personality. For the student of personality, even if the event could be proved, it would be quite irrelevant.

As a matter of fact, as we have seen in the study of the sources, our historical knowledge of the life of Jesus begins with his coming to the baptism of John. The "history" of the events surrounding his birth would probably not have made more exciting reading than of any other child born of parents in Nazareth or Bethlehem. It was what Jesus *became* that made his birth significant, not the extraordinary accompaniments to the event. He had to strive and overcome and make his own the will of God.

In a remarkable way the two contradictory birth accounts, which no ingenuity can harmonize, express two of the greatest values in the coming of Jesus. Legend says he was found not by the princes and the mighty, but by lowly shepherds, who came to the stable where alone there was room for him. Though not accepted by his own people, the Wise Men came from afar to

72

Jesus with their treasures. Matthew, the most Judaic Gospel of all, not only ends with the great missionary commission out of the experience of the post-Pauline church, but begins with this missionary document, the coming of the Magi.

These were stories that were early told about Jesus. We do not need to believe that they were events that happened in just the way related, for angels do not belong to the pages of "history." Here is "truth" which is greater than fact. Most young people will come to recognize it as such when they come to an age to distinguish legend from history. The problem arises from the dogmatic insistence upon fact on the part of a well-intentioned teacher who has not himself learned to distinguish it from interpretation.

In the accounts of the life of Jesus we must distinguish again and again between history and interpretation. When a historian evaluates the sources, he does not compromise between conflicting reports. He must to the best of his ability choose one or the other. As long as a religious teacher takes as his task merely the exposition of a book, such as the Gospel of Matthew, he will face little difficulty. But if he really desires to set forth the true historical character of Jesus, he cannot treat legend and history upon the same plane. Did John protest against baptizing Jesus, as Matthew represents, or is the account in Mark the true one?[13] It is manifestly dishonest to teach the story as it stands in Matthew if historical criticism has demonstrated to our satisfaction that Mark gives the truer account of the event. We cannot exalt the virtue of honesty if we turn aside from

[13] Matthew 3. 14; Mark 1. 9.

such a problem with the comforting excuse that we do not want our students to question the Holy Scriptures. Is it better to lead them to doubt the honesty of teachers of religion? The average teacher, who cannot be abreast of historical scholarship, will in perfectly good conscience often make false assertions. Ignorance is always pardonable in such a case. What is unpardonable is the assumption that we may aid in the progress of Truth by hiding truth.

Instead of dealing with other small concrete cases of this sort we will turn at once to a different phase of the problem, that is, a whole incident which appears legendary. The best illustration is the transfiguration. It is quite out of the question to make anything as "history" out of the report of the transforming of Jesus into a dazzling appearance, and his conversation with worthies of by-gone centuries. Some look upon it as a visionary experience of the disciples. Others believe that a resurrection appearance of Jesus has been transferred in the tradition to his earthly life. Others remind us of the use by Jewish teachers of "midrash," defined by Doctor Driver as "an imaginative development of a thought or theme suggested by scripture, especially a didactic or homiletic exposition or edifying religious story."[14] They suggest that the transfiguration is an early Christian midrash to set forth in pictorial form the discovery by the disciples that Jesus was more than the law, as symbolized by Moses, and more than the prophets, as symbolized by Elias. If that be the correct interpretation, its value remains, but nothing is to be gained by insisting that an "event" took place that defies all inherent probability.

---

[14] Driver, S. R., *Literature of the Old Testament*, 5th ed., p. 497.

Finally, there comes under this problem the use of stories in the fourth Gospel which we have come to believe, as a result of comparative study, must be interpretative rather than factual in character. Most acute does this become in relation to the discourses in which the religious reflection of the evangelist has so overladen such sayings as may have come through tradition that it is difficult to claim any as genuine words of the historical Jesus. We must never forget that we have a religious objective in endeavoring to show men Jesus. If we share in the interpretations of John, we cannot be satisfied with simply stripping them off as later accretions. Probably the best way to avoid a disgusting and misleading pedantry is to lead the student always to the fourth Gospel as to a religious interpretation rather than a historical life. Our primary purpose is not to see how often his story deviates from that in Mark, but how far his evaluation is one in which we can share. It will be profitless to debate with a class whether Jesus was actually called "Saviour of the world" in his lifetime by Samaritan villagers. What our pupils need to discover is how he may merit that title to-day. By focusing attention upon what the Gospel of John is, we may avoid unnecessary explanations concerning what it is not. Much that is secondary for history may be primary in religious value. Legend may teach truth so long as it is not confused with fact.

GOSPEL ATTITUDES TOWARD JEWS

A third problem is presented by the anti-Jewish bias of our New Testament writings. How will this affect the achievement of our objective of brotherhood? A large and significant group, especially in our larger centers, are Jews. Will understanding and sympathetic relations with them be fostered by a study of the Gospels? The death of Jesus is the focal point of attention throughout the New Testament. Despite the fact that he was "crucified under Pontius Pilate," there is an increasing tendency in those writings to throw all of the blame upon the Jews. For centuries in the ghettoes of Europe the finger of hatred has been pointed at the Jew who killed our Lord. When a spectacular moving picture depicting the death of "The King of Kings" was displayed, it is reported that New York Jews secured the excision of inserts calculated to awaken anti-semitic feeling. In defense of the movie magnates, it must be recognized that the expressions were drawn directly from the Bible.

When this problem was first raised with one long-time Sunday-school attendant, it was waived aside as the figment of the imagination of a scholar engrossed in his books. It was contended by this objector that in the actual teaching of our church schools the Jews of New Testament times are such unreal and far-away characters that no pupil would think of connecting them with semitic boys and girls in his own school. Doubtless that is often the case, and such an opinion represents a damaging indictment of our teaching. But the problem does exist even if one resurrects none of the characters in the New Testament from the pages of the Book.

The character of Jesus himself is deeply involved by the harsh attitudes represented. We *say* that the high point of his teaching is the injunction of love toward enemies. But words are relatively cheap. Did Jesus love his enemies? At once the beautiful prayer in Luke comes to our minds, "Father, forgive them; for they

know not what they do.''[15]   We are inclined to have little
patience with the protest that it was only intended for the
Roman soldiers, the blind instruments of military authority.   But there is no such easy reply to the word of
the textual student who informs us that these words are
not found in many of the earliest manuscripts, and the
consensus of scholarship is that they must be set aside
as an early insertion into the text.   With that doubtful
verse excluded, what is the attitude in the rest of the
Gospels?   "Hypocrites," "offspring of vipers," "whited
sepulchers," "blind guides," and the like are not the
vocabulary which we are accustomed to associate with
the feeling of love.   Montefiori, one of the most fair-
minded of liberal Jewish scholars, is led to assert that if
Jesus had shown any of the love toward the Pharisees
that he revealed toward the publicans and sinners, the
former might have listened to his message more cordially.
Is there any evidence, we are asked, that Jesus did show
love to his own enemies?   We are not concerned with a
dogma of the sinlessness of Jesus.   Certainly, the challenge in John 8. 46, "Which of you convicteth me of sin?"
would have brought forth the angry retort from the
Pharisees that Jesus was a terrible sinner, for he actually
commanded a man to do work on the Sabbath day.   We
are concerned with the nobility of his character, and we
cannot exalt him unless we can believe in his magnanimity.

We have had occasion in another connection to bring
out the fundamentally different point of view of Jesus
and the Pharisees, despite their agreement on a multitude
of individual questions, such as the resurrection.   If we
can trust the book of Acts, the earliest opposition to the

[15] Luke 23. 34.

77

believers in the messiahship of Jesus came from the Sadducees.[16]   It was when differences over the law became prominent that the Pharisees joined in the persecution.[17] This cleavage grew wider and wider, particularly as a result of the work of Paul.   A message which proclaimed that Christ was the end of the law could not fail to inflame the zealots for the Torah.   However glorious as expressions of Christian belief Galatians and Romans may be, the fact remains that they convinced very few Jews. Instead, more and more riots and disturbances were incited by them.   Synagogue was arrayed in hostility against the church.   It is amid such an atmosphere that our Gospels were written.

A comparison of Mark with the later Gospels reveals a growing tendency to identify all opponents of Jesus as Pharisees.   Three verses suffice for his woes upon them, while in Matthew and Luke the polemic has grown to a whole chapter.[18]   Much of this is doubtless early tradition, but the venomous formulation has been made by a church opposed by hostile Pharisaic leadership.   This development is easiest to follow in the story of the trial.   Luke, who in Acts is careful to show that Roman officials are uniformly friendly, goes beyond the Markan picture of a compliant Pilate and makes that brutal Roman official affirm three times, "I find no fault in him."[19]   John goes still further in this direction and has the high priests swear allegiance to Cæsar.[20]   In Matthew, Pilate washes his hands of the whole matter while the Jews voluntarily

[16] Acts 4. 1; 5. 17.
[17] Acts 6. 11; 15. 5; 23. 9.
[18] Mark 12. 38-40; Matthew 23. 1-36; Luke 11. 39-54.
[19] Luke 23. 4, 14, 22.
[20] John 19. 15.

assume all responsibility, shouting, "His blood be on us, and on our children."[21] We see here the growing desire to justify their hatred toward the Jews, and at least in Luke-Acts, to assure Roman political officials that Christians have always been considered politically innocuous.

When we look beneath this bias of the early church, we discover that all of the relations of Jesus with the Pharisees were by no means strained or hostile. He is often represented as a dinner guest in their homes. Pharisees warn him that his life is in danger.[22] Some of the discussions given a controversial character by the evangelists reveal, in fact, a friendly discussion concerning religious and moral duties.[23] That we have not more evidence of this kind is due to the fragmentary and tendential character of our tradition. We do wish that some incident of loving concern for a Pharisee had been preserved, but we are not warranted in concluding that nothing of the kind ever happened. On the contrary, what more poignant words of love for one's people have been uttered than, "O Jerusalem, Jerusalem, thou that killest the prophets, . . . how often would I have gathered thy children together, even as a hen gathereth her chickens under her wings, and ye would not!" The nation so tenderly addressed included Pharisee and Sadducee as well as publican and sinner.

Nor need we be embarrassed by the outspoken attacks of Jesus upon the Pharisees. Modern Jewish apologists have been unduly sensitive about them because of the false assumption of many Christians that Pharisees were

[21] Matthew 27. 25.
[22] Luke 13. 31.
[23] Mark 12. 28ff.

79

identical with "hypocrites." It should not be forgotten
that the Pharisees were the most religious and conscientious group in Judaism. They alone survived, with
a vital religious faith, the terrible catastrophe of the fall
of Jerusalem in 70 A. D. and the later carnage under
Hadrian. Why, however, should we hesitate to believe
that among these were many whose piety was a pretense
and a mockery? We need only look within our Christian
churches to feel the appropriateness of many of the
stinging words of Jesus. There are few more valuable
passages than these pictures of the "perils of piety," so
long as we apply them to ourselves, and do not assume
that they are exclusively applicable to Jews in Palestine.
Among the Pharisees there was evidenced the aberrations
of piety almost inevitable in a group setting themselves
apart as more religious than ordinary men. The lash
of the prophet falls upon the conformist religious leaders,
for he feels that they present the greatest obstacles to
the renovation of religion. History again and again
demonstrates how suspicious toward outside leadership
these can be. Hence, Jesus could hardly avoid the feeling
that though he shared much in common with the Pharisees, nevertheless they presented the greatest obstacle to
his work.

These passages will be a reminder to us that Jesus
considered hypocrisy and formalism among the greatest
of sins. The words are not to be looked upon as the
condemnation of a race, but of the sins to which the
religious of all times are most susceptible. Our students
must see these words translated into modern situations
and read, "Woe unto you, stewards and vestrymen!"
While Jesus insisted that we should not usurp the divine

prerogative of judgment, this did not mean we should remain opinionless.[24] The religious do not need to be reminded of the love of God toward them. They need to realize that the wrath of God rests upon every cloak of piety. Countless Jews stand not one whit behind Christians in the sincerity of their worship. Hypocrisy is our common foe, and one that is to be feared more than flagrant ungodliness, for it is so insidious and deceiving. In this warfare, the youth of our day has every sympathy and interest.

DOES GOD REALLY CARE?

A fourth problem is of a more definitely theological character. Particularly for young children, the favorite theme of religious educators is "God's loving care." Outside of the Christmas and Easter stories, no gospel passages are used more frequently than the few extolling God's care in nature. "Behold the birds of the heaven, that they sow not, neither do they reap, nor gather into barns; and your heavenly Father feedeth them."[25] "Are not two sparrows sold for a penny? and not one of them shall fall on the ground without your Father: but the very hairs of your head are all numbered. Fear not therefore: ye are of more value than many sparrows."[26]

No one would dispute the beauty of these verses, nor the importance of the theme of God's loving care. But teachers must consider whether they are laying the foundation for a sound faith or whether they are cultivating a "Pollyanna" type of religion. Will pupils later

---

[24] Matthew 7. 1.
[25] Matthew 6. 26; Luke 12. 24.
[26] Matthew 10. 29-31; Luke 12. 6-7.

face the alternative of disillusionment before the realities of life, or retirement to an unreal world where, ostrich-like, they ignore the facts?

The problem is twofold in character. The ultimate question is whether it is true to the facts of the world in which we live. Into such a final question of faith it is impossible here to enter. If we should become convinced that such a faith is unjustified, the issue would become part of the problem of the authority of Jesus. The more immediate aspect concerns the interpretation of these verses in the light of the *whole* teaching of Jesus. Did Jesus hold a naïve faith in the eternal goodness of things? What did God's loving care mean to him? Did it signify that God would protect his children from all harm? Did Jesus really believe that prayer was an unfailing means of getting what we desire?[27]

As a matter of fact, nothing can hide the intense realism of Jesus. Whether we call the expressions of God's care poetic exaggerations or childlike trust, in any case they present but one side of his teaching. Jesus was under no illusion concerning the reality of a desperate life struggle. He summoned men not to a pleasant Utopia but to rigorous sacrifice. Other apocalyptists believed that during the woes which should come on the earth in the last time the pious would be miraculously preserved. Not so Jesus. He foretold suffering, perse-cution, hardship, and even death to his followers. It is true that our Gospels reflect in their wording the actual persecutions which believers had already undergone at the time they were written. There is no way to disen-tangle these secondary formulations from the original

[27] Mark 11. 24; Luke 11. 9ff.

prophecies of Jesus. But it would be difficult to deny
that he did expect that others too would have to tread
the difficult road of sacrifice. God was a God of loving
care, but that did not save any from family opposition,
from social discrimination, or from suffering and death.[28]

Can we teach such a religion to children? Do we lay
a foundation for such a faith with delightful stories about
God's love for the birds and the flowers and the animals?
Does the religious educator desire a basis for comfortable
optimism and gracious amiability, or the rigorous heroism
which led Jesus to a cross? Do we want boys and girls
to believe that there are angels in heaven who guard
over their safety, or that to live in this world in conscientious loyalty to highest principles is only possible
at genuine cost? Such are some of the questions upon
which every teacher must ponder.

Some accept the conclusion that we do live in a hostile
world, in which we strive to carve out our ideals. The
logic of such a premise would rule out all lessons about
God's care in nature. They must accept the opposition
between man and his best ideals on the one hand, and a
world of nature which is utterly indifferent thereto. The
best Christian thought, however, has always insisted,
"This is my Father's world." It was not made by some
lower deity, nor is it simply an impersonal mechanism.
But we cannot deduce from an abstract belief in God's
loving care what we think it might mean in life. It
appears that a friendly universe does provide for infinite
risk and heroic struggle. The religious life can be interpreted truly under no other terms.

Hence the teacher must remind his pupils that God's

---

[28] Matthew 10. 34ff.; Luke 12. 51; 14. 26ff.

loving care for Jesus did not save him from the cruel cross. Neither will it save us from bearing our real crosses. The Father's world is one where every good must be won at the cost of sacrifice amid risk of at least temporary defeat and failure. An easy time is the last thing that a follower of Jesus can expect. Ours is a real struggle. But it was the faith of Jesus that we strive not alone, but "My Father worketh even until now, and I work."

Our problem is how to be true to the total faith of Jesus. We only wish that we knew how Jesus himself dealt with small children. We feel certain that when he took them in his arms and blessed them, he tried to make them realize that "underneath and round about were the everlasting arms." But did he say nothing equivalent to, "He that doth not take his cross and follow after me is not worthy of me"? Very soon he must have made clear that God did not save from physical peril those who loved him. If we are to be true to him, we must join from the earliest beginning childlike trust and heroic struggle.

The Authority of Jesus

The most important and fundamental problem of all in teaching the life of Jesus concerns the authority which we can ascribe to him. We say that we desire our pupils to look to him as Lord and Master. The last retreat of the authoritarian appeal has been to Jesus. The Protestant Reformers revolted from the conception of an authoritative church, and set in its place an infallible Bible. Slowly the acids of historical criticism have dissipated this illusory infallibility. Many modern Christians have insisted, instead, that our authority lies in a living person, not a dead book. Jesus is our authoritative guide to life, and the final appeal in religion. This has been the case no less among those who have quietly laid aside orthodox dogmas of the incarnation as among those who cling tenaciously to traditional theories.

From two sides, however, belief in the authority of Jesus has been questioned. Many are definitely repudiating the whole authoritarian concept. The only authorities for which they have any use are specialists in the knowledge of facts. They exercise no dominion over us except in their greater familiarity with the discoveries in a particular field. There is nothing "final" about any knowledge, and nothing "infallible" about any authority. Every belief must be submitted to continuous criticism and renewed verification. When we leave the realms of fact for those of appreciation and evaluation, "authorities" have even less place. There is no appeal beyond the impression of truth made upon the individual. Jesus, therefore, may be helpful as a "way," but there is no authority which can assure us of the "truth." That must be continuously pursued.

Furthermore, it is questioned whether Jesus actually is an infallible guide to the highest way of life. The geometry of Euclid is as true as it ever was, but what authority can we assign to a man who believed in demonology, was subject to the limited mental horizon of an ancient people, and in particular shared in their apocalyptic dreams? Naturally, at this point, interpretations differ. There are those who insist that Jesus simply accommodated himself to the beliefs of his people about demons and the authorship of various Old Testament writings. In particular, they insist that the apocalyptic framework was simply a current vehicle of thought that Jesus "adopted" in order to speak to his age, but, of course, he himself stood above its fantasies. Behind all such apologetic case-pleading lies the implied belief that if it be granted that Jesus did heartily believe such outworn conceptions, it would be all over with the ascription to him of a unique authority.

It should be noted that learned theologians in Germany are insisting to-day that belief in Jesus as the incarnation of God rests in no way upon demonstrating that his words offer for us to-day an infallible guide to life.[29] They consider that the appeal to the religious personality of Jesus is a great mistake of liberal theology. We must, rather, accept the fact of the great deed for man's redemption which God performed in Christ on faith in the apostolic witness. These theologians do not expect to present a Jesus insulated from the thought of his time. That would rob him of significance as much as removing a man's brain from the living organism of which it is a part would destroy its power. They seek to establish the faith that "God was in Christ reconciling the world unto himself," and hold that that belief is not connected at all with whether Jesus affords a solution for any or all of our modern problems, or whether his "way of life" is either feasible or authoritative.

The intensity of the problem of the authority of Jesus arises for us out of the lingering influence of the Ritschlian theology. Rauschenbusch,[30] Kirby Page,[31] and countless others who followed in the train of the "back-to-Christ movement," have been insisting upon the contrast

---

[29] Brunner, E., *Der Mittler*.

[30] Rauschenbusch, Walter, *Jesus Christ and the Social Question*.

[31] Page, Kirby, *Jesus or Christianity*.

between Jesus himself and the historic Christian Church which has appropriated his name. A comparison of such books with that which we believe to be the assured findings of historical scholarship will reveal that they are dealing with a far from authentic Jesus. Nevertheless, one side of their contention is true. Historic Christianity did not set up an authoritative Jesus whose way was to be followed. Many of our expounders of the social gospel have laid this as an indictment against the church of the past. The indictment contains great truth. But is the assumption upon which it rests correct? In what sense does Jesus offer guidance to a continuing society? Was not an other-worldly redemption rooted in Jesus fully as much as our modern social-service enthusiasm? Does none of the wisdom of the ages lie behind the failure to realize all of the ideal of Jesus? Is all of the contrast between him and our civilization due to human perverseness, and the faltering loyalty of his followers?

The problem is not one of abstract possibilities, but of fact. Who was Jesus? What authority do we and can we give to this historical character? It ought to present no difficulty that Jesus does not turn out to be an authority on questions of science and history. Since infallibility is claimed for the Pope only when speaking *ex cathedra* upon questions of faith and morals, Protestants should have no objection to the restriction of the authority of Jesus to such realms. But our really vital problem lies right here. Did not Jesus forbid categorically all divorce? Yet liberal Christians who appeal to his authority oftentimes call those bodies who cling to this "law" illiberal and blind to facts. Did not Jesus exalt

"Blessed are you hungry, for you shall be satisfied"

poverty and warn against riches? Yet in the authority of his name we appeal for the abolition of poverty. Did he not assume a future punishment, while increasing numbers feel that the idea is unworthy of a good God? Finally, if he actually did cherish the delusion that a new world was about to dawn, is it not absurd to talk about him as our absolute authority? His final appeal was not to love, but to an arbitrary intervention of power.

We believe that this last question contains the heart of the whole problem, and the answer to the ones before it. Upon this primary aspect we will focus our attention. We will not repeat the evidence in the reconstruction of the portrait of Jesus for the vitality of his apocalyptic expectations. As was affirmed by Friedrich Heiler, the great historian of prayer, "The recognition of the eschatological character of Jesus' gospel is the Copernican achievement of modern theology."[32] As cautious a student as H. Holtzmann sums it up, "The eschatological perspective of Jesus knows as the last phase a powerful act of omnipotence on the part of God, intervening from above and cutting short the whole course of the world; an act whereby human co-operation appeared to be shut out, and every bridge between the present and the future broken off."[33]

There is no denial that such a belief is quite foreign to our modern point of view. Millennial expectations survive chiefly where biblicism has not been contaminated by science. The only other exception lies in revolutionary socialism, which has its own quite secular apocalyptic messianism. Instead of trying to whittle down the extent

---

[32] Heiler, Fr., *Der Katholizismus*, p. 3.
[33] Holtzmann, H., *Neutestamentliche Theologie*, I, p. 285. 2d ed., 1910.

of influence of this alien conception, would it not be a better approach to ask concerning the positive values which it may hold for us? When we consider ancient ideas, we should not ask if we can hold them to-day, for rarely is that entirely possible. The vital question concerns the motives that led to their formulation and the truths that found imperfect expression in them. We fail to think historically if we simply affirm in condescension that they were mistaken. We will confine ourselves to two elements of value which it seems to us should appeal to most people.

(1) Apocalyptic cuts the nerve of all pantheism by its proclamation of the *coming* reign of God. The God of some of the apocalyptists was almost entirely transcendent. This was not so in Jesus, for whom the lilies of the field were an expression of the beauty of God. We are grateful to a modern theology which emphasizes the immanence of God, but important streams of thought are insisting that we have gone too far. They say that we must reclaim the complete "otherness" of God. Apocalyptic does not permit any identification of the will of God with the present evil age, nor does the evolution of its present potentialities exhaust his power. It is monistic enough to assert the ultimate triumph of the good, but it is pluralistic enough to take seriously the fact of evil. The apocalyptic expectation was one endeavor to unite these two realities—actual evil to be overcome on the one hand, and the holy will of the determiner of destiny on the other. The Kingdom expectation did not arise from the feverish fanaticism of unbalanced minds, as it might appear to us to-day. It arose from an earnest belief in God's holy will. God must vindicate

his ethical purpose in a great act of redemption. Jesus purged this expectation of every element of revenge and from its association with exclusive national glory. It meant for him that the final sovereignty of God's holy will was certain, and that was other than any merely relative human ideal.

(2) But, most important of all, the apocalyptic hope was the *historical condition* for the rise of the heroic ethic of Jesus. It is a mistake to consider his ethic as ascetic, but it does stand in marked contrast to the world-affirming ideal of Greece. Renunciation for its own sake was never counseled, but Jesus did show a reckless disregard for the consequences in his unconditional pursuit of God's ideal. May it not be that Wundt was right when he spoke from the psychological point of view, "Ideals can only arise as ideas in whose reality or realization we can believe"?[34] The real interim ethic is not that of Jesus but that which exists because of the "hardness of men's hearts." Practical compromises with the institutions of this world are necessarily relative. An ethic that can claim absolute validity will arise in connection with the vision of an ideal world. "Jesus did not build up his ethic with a view to solving the problem of how to organize a perfectly ethical society, but he preaches the ethic of men who together strive to attain to a perfect yielding of themselves to the will of God."[35] Instead therefore of invalidating the ethics of Jesus, as is often claimed, the apocalyptic expectation intensified its radical character. It provided the historical circumstances under which he set forth his vision of absolute values.

[34] Wundt, W., *System der Ethik*, p. 322.
[35] Schweitzer, A., *Christianity and the Religions of the World*, p. 36.

90

Historically speaking, the problem of the delayed Parousia, or second coming, as it has been called, was met in the Christian experience of a present, living Christ. It is, of course, a mistake to correct the records of the synoptic Gospels by this later experience. But the Johannine solution does indicate to us where the ultimate authority must always lie, and that is in religious experience. Experience does not demand an infallible, external authority, which, if we possessed it, would only stultify initiative. The corporate experience of humanity is its own authority. Jesus can save no one from the necessity of using his own mind. We need no external claims to bolster the appeal which he actually does make to the hearts of men.

Our discussion of the authority of Jesus thus far may seem to have raised many more questions than it has answered. It has dealt with questions which "the man on the street" is hardly aware of, and has apparently left almost untouched those vital issues connected with the disregard of Jesus in so many spheres of our practical life. But they are the questions which will be raised with fuller knowledge, and the religious teacher must be ready to meet them or face embarrassing discomfiture. Men and women will profess to be greatly shocked at the admission that Jesus was mistaken at any point. Nothing is gained by trying to deny that Jesus shared in the world-view of the time. But we must focus attention upon the abiding and really important questions. Was Jesus mistaken in the character of God, and in his evaluation of persons? Was he in error concerning the primacy of love and good will? Was he an impractical idealist when he chose the way of the cross?

Our answers to such questions can be supported by no
external validation. The heart that is touched by his is
the sole justification of his authority. It will avail
naught to argue the case through ten pages or through
one hundred. In our attempt to see Jesus as he was
we have listened to his real claim. Further case-pleading
could only repeat what has already been said in the last
chapter. The sway which he can exercise over the souls
of men depends upon the inherent value of the life he lived
and the words he spoke. Individuals have remained and
will remain untouched. But the collective experience of
the race is eloquent in testifying to the adequacy of his
leadership.

After all, what experience craves is *adequate inspiration*.
"The authority of Jesus" is a useful concept only as we
translate it in terms of present experience under his
inspiration. What commands our loyalty is not an exact
code, a body of teachings, a set of ready-made solutions,
but an inspiring leader, a great personality, one whose
example will fire us to go and do likewise. What we need
is an assurance that along this *way* is the largest life.
We could not use the final map. If there is any greater
inspiration to heroic faith, confident hope, and self-giving
love, we are not aware of it. The authority of Jesus lies
in his infinite capacity to stir the enthusiasms of men, and
enlist their loyalty to their noblest ideals. Neither the
historian nor the theologian can demonstrate that authority. It can only be proved by the appeal which the
Jesus we teach makes to the hearts of men.

CHAPTER V

WHAT HAS JESUS FOR DIFFERENT AGES?

THE principle of the grading of lesson materials in church schools has now become firmly established, although in actual practice many compromises are often necessary. We cannot treat the problems of teaching the life of Jesus as a unity, for the interests of small children, adolescents, and adults are not the same. In carrying out the principle of a life-centered curriculum, attention must be given to the needs of the pupil rather than to the dissemination of a given body of facts. Hence the use that is made of the life of Jesus will vary with the age group. It will be convenient in the treatment in this chapter to follow in the main the accepted departmental divisions of the church school.

FOR SMALL CHILDREN

With small children it is an axiom that teaching must be in story form. Abstract material has no place whatever. What is more, the incident should relate itself to the life experience of the child. But the first difficulty in the use of the Bible with small children is that it is an adult book and deals with adult experiences. Though Jesus took little children in his arms and blessed them, the tradition does not recount what he said. Many vivid incidents from his life are preserved for us, but they are not childhood experiences. Increasing numbers are doubting that information about adults affords religious edu-

cation for childhood. "It is evident that the full presentation, even of the simplest of the synoptic Gospels,
cannot be adequately appreciated before childhood's
days are well over. It is quite possible and even probable
that most of the material of the first three Gospels was
derived from the catechetical instruction of the early
church; but if so, it was certainly not the instruction of
children."[1]

It is a well-established principle among elementary
teachers that the smaller the child, the fewer the biblical
stories that will be used. Our best Beginners courses are
built around the experiences of the home and the family,
food and animals, the seasons, and especially the great
religious festivals of Christmas and Easter. Not the
slightest attempt is made to teach any portion of the
Bible consecutively. A few striking memory verses are
used, such as "Your Heavenly Father feedeth them,"
and a few incidents that may be expected to appeal to
childhood.

Four or five lessons may well be given each Advent
season to the beautiful stories which surround the coming
of God's most precious gift to the world. The story of
the humble birth, the visit of the lowly shepherds, and the
homage of distant peoples symbolize in vivid narrative
form much of the meaning of the whole life of Jesus.
When so many influences conspire to secularize the Christmas season, the church school must place renewed emphasis
upon Him who has given the day its name. Of somewhat
secondary importance for our use are the Annunciation,
the presentation in the Temple, and the flight into Egypt,

---

[1] Jones, J. M., *The New Testament in Modern Education.* Hodder and
Stoughton, London. Quoted by special permission.

but in them all are ideas that can be understood by the kindergarten child—the mother's joy in God's precious gift; from earliest birth the child belongs to God; through parents and loved ones we are protected from danger even as helpless babes. Re-enforced by pictures, professedly of the creative imagination of our artists, the meaning of the coming of Jesus may be conveyed through the artistic stories early circulated among the believers in Palestine.

Our canonical Gospels report only one incident from the boyhood of Jesus—the trip to the Feast at Jerusalem, which the lad made the year before he should take upon himself the full responsibility of obedience to the law. Religious educators, however, have not been satisfied with our ignorance. Most of our modern courses have inserted imaginative incidents illustrative of the obedience, helpfulness, and kindness of the lad in the carpenter's home of Nazareth. Most of them are in far different taste than the crass miracles in which the writers of the apocryphal Gospels of the second and third centuries delighted. The chapter on the boyhood of Jesus in Doctor Glover's *The Jesus of History* will reveal how from the later preaching of Jesus we may reconstruct with a high degree of probability experiences of his boyhood. Nevertheless many conscientious teachers will prefer to preface the narration of such incidents with such a phrase as, "This is a story that is related *about* Jesus."

The man Jesus cannot be presented as an example for little children. Nor will such a term as "Saviour" bear any possible meaning to their present experience. Jesus must come to them as one to love and admire because he went about doing good in deeds of kindness. Naturally, the incident of blessing the little children will be the one used most frequently. When we realize how unique it is among the authentic traditions of great religious founders, when we discover how ready the evangelists were to turn words of Jesus about actual children into sayings about childlike believers, we are assured that the picture of Jesus as the friend of children is not the figment of a pious imagination. The Johannine interpretation of Jesus as the Good Shepherd is almost as striking in its appeal.

Most of the stories of helpfulness have some miraculous element, but for the very smallest children that need not present a problem. The author can testify to the number of times a four-year-old in his home called for the story about Jesus and the fishermen, and the story of the boy that was sick (nobleman's son). However, when we consider all of the interests that come close to the child's experience, it is of doubtful value to extend the list to include many healing stories, even during the primary period. Attitudes and habits to be cultivated in the children may present the real objective to be sought from the use of some. The healing of the ten lepers may be simply a background for a lesson in thankfulness. One recent course offers a lesson bearing the suggestive title, "When Jesus Came to Supper," which at once suggests the transition from behavior at a first-century meal in Palestine to the coming of guests into a twentieth-century home in America.

So far we have been thinking of the place of Jesus in the curriculum of the church kindergarten. We must not overlook the Bible stories read by the mother in the home. Here a somewhat wider range of choice may be made from the versions retold in simple language understandable to childhood. Educators will hardly need to be reminded that the Authorized Version is not in the vocabulary of a child, and for many years Bible stories should be retold in simpler form. The individual mother may well experiment with stories that would hardly be chosen for use in the church school.

Easter is the other great seasonal festival with a biblical connection. Experienced students of child life, however, turn preferably to the awakening of nature to bring home its story of the triumph of life. The closing events in the life of Jesus present a compelling drama, but it has been too readily assumed by some that the story of the events would be helpful to the smallest children. The triumphal entry may afford a chance to stress the leadership of Jesus, a leadership to which later experience must largely give content. The crucifixion, with its gruesome death scene, however, is hardly to be emphasized as yet. The resurrection of Jesus can hardly be discussed with even much older children except under such materialistic symbols as a vacant tomb and a revivified body. There will be many who will question the wisdom of this. In some of our newer courses the beautiful story of the walk to Emmaus is used to convey the idea of a present Jesus who is with us. It will depend upon the point of view of the individual teacher whether she desires to encourage belief in the ever-present Jesus or the God whom Jesus called Father. Obviously, both the problems and significance of Easter have meaning only for more mature experience. Nature rather than the Bible will probably for some time offer the more understandable symbols.

THE PRIMARY YEARS

The primary years present a developing period when imagination is active, reasoning power begins to appear, and when imitation is strong. School brings widening interests; experience begins to reach beyond the home to a larger neighborhood; the new associations bring perplexing problems and fresh, compelling interests. Nevertheless, there is no real change in the principle of presenting the life of Jesus. There is little point in attempting a consecutive list of stories, for neither history nor biography is as yet a significant concept. We will still use isolated incidents that may begin, "Once upon a time." The point to be raised is not whether they come in order in the life of Jesus, but whether they relate themselves to genuine child interests and needs of the moment. The great Christian festivals will continue to have the same emphasis, but at other times such stories as are chosen from the life of Jesus will be interspersed among Old Testament stories, or extrabiblical incidents, as the consideration of child problems may demand.

Hence the stories will not be used primarily to give factual information about Jesus. In most cases the objective will be found in something closely related to child needs. The two points of view may be illustrated by quoting titles of different lessons using the same biblical materials. In one course there is offered a lesson upon "Restoring Life to a Little Girl." In another, the same incident is made the basis for a discussion of "Never Too Hurried to Help." One is factual; the other seeks more directly to inculcate helpfulness. Or we may turn to the incident of the healing of the paralytic in

Mark 2. 1-12. In one lesson it is used to show "The Power of Jesus to Forgive Sins." In another it becomes the basis for a study on "Helping Build a Healthy City."

The changed point of view has become an accepted axiom with many curriculum makers and lesson writers. By using the gospel incidents in this way we not only carry out improved educational procedure, but we cultivate a familiarity with the stories from which a knowledge of Jesus will gradually be built up. Sometimes we wonder, however, if there has not been a doubtful compromise between educational method and the widespread expectation on the part of parents and church-school teachers that the Bible should afford the major part of the curriculum material. Farfetched analogies are sometimes drawn in the endeavor to relate more stories to childhood experiences than can legitimately be done. When the preparations for the triumphal entry become the occasion for a lesson on "An Errand for Jesus," many will wonder if it would not be better to choose a story more closely related to the intended application. It is far from certain that respect for the Bible will be inculcated by dragging in verses from the second chapter of Luke for a lesson on "Getting Ready for Vacation." No rule, of course, can be laid down, for judgments will differ upon individual cases. Most of such incongruities arise from a compromise between two conflicting objectives.

Among the best incidents to relate are those which Jesus himself told, rather than events from his own life. The matchless parables that have been preserved reveal that he was a peerless story-teller. We do not wonder that the common people heard him gladly or that children stayed to listen to him speak. How could helpfulness be better set forth than in the person of the good Samaritan? If we want a story to illustrate "Doing Our Best," we may well turn to the parable of the talents. The picture of the forgiving father in the fifteenth chapter of Luke has a universal appeal. When we come, however, to such a parable as that of the sower, while the events are within child experience, the same can hardly be said for the application.

There are also incidents from the life of Jesus that may be fruitfully applied even for primary children. Jesus' need of prayer links him with the youngest child of God. If keeping the Sabbath day was a problem to first-century Jews, so is the wise use of Sunday to-day, even for small children. If forgiveness was not easy for a grown man like Peter, neither does it come naturally to a self-assertive youngster. If Jesus found it advantageous to discuss humility, with illustrations drawn from the formal dinners of society, we should not hesitate to include "Whom to Invite to a Party" in the list of themes we will discuss in our church school. Obviously, this is not teaching the life of Jesus, but it is something better. It is teaching *children*, and in a manner which appears to agree with the way in which he taught.

The Needs of the Junior

We cannot enter upon a detailed presentation of the characteristics of that period of exuberant energy through which juniors pass. Readers are rather directed to the manuals which survey child psychology, but, better still, to the close observation of actual children. Psychologists as well as theologians are sometimes given to affirming more than they can fully prove. If human nature is at least in a measure a product, our descriptive psychologies must be rewritten as our environment changes. The physical development of children may not differ from what it was fifty years ago, but even here improvement in health education has left its mark. Outstanding inventions do transform the child because they change the environment in which he forms his habits and to which he responds. Problems of sex must be faced much earlier than in former years, and it is clear that older statistics on the age of conversion are no longer accurate.

We will not attempt to depict a detailed picture of the developing child, for obviously there are many of his needs that will not call for an appeal to Jesus. It is instructive to turn to the later Epistles of the New Testament, where we are struck, in the midst of extremely elementary moral instruction, with the paucity of references to him whom they called Lord. Before the new converts could rise to a high level of Christian living they must first become decent, respectable men and women. Many of the moral and religious needs of our boys and girls are not to be met by a stress upon that which is specifically Christian and distinctive in our faith. The church school must inculcate the pagan virtues as well as the Christian graces.

We will therefore restrict our attention throughout to those needs of childhood and adolescence which seem to call for more than an incidental treatment of the life of Jesus. It is assumed that for all ages there will be the use of gospel incidents such as described for primary children. When, however, should there be presented a connected account of his life? Many feel that since at the close of the junior years the children of Christian parents should be ready for a "decision for Christ" and member-ship in his church, these years should include a life of Jesus. But are they ready yet to study history as such? Since our sources really do not permit a chronological account, our newer and better courses are shortening the period for such a study. The weeks between Christmas and Easter afford ample time to sketch the main outline of his career in so far as a ten- or eleven-year-old child can fruitfully use that information. But if we desire to leave the impression of a historical life, we must accept the limitations which a critical study of history impose upon us. Many will feel that Johannine incidents should not be included in the fashion of the harmonistic lives of forty years ago. Teachers should be provided with modern helps based upon our present knowledge. They should be frankly told that many widely read lives of Christ, such as those by Stalker and Edersheim, are no more valuable authorities than the geographies published at the same time.

Jesus, the active hero, is the figure which should be vital to the junior. Such lesson titles as "A Tireless Worker," "Taking a Difficult Stand," and "Jesus and His Enemies" indicate the kind of topics that will touch the most responsive chord. True stories are his demand now, for he can distinguish clearly between fact and fiction. Hence, if we should use such an incident as the raising of Jairus' daughter, a wise teacher would probably indicate that it was a story early told about Jesus by people who had been deeply impressed with his kindly helpfulness. Now many could read with sufficient facility a connected story of Jesus for children. Would that we had an ade-quate version to put in their hands!

The Problems of Adolescents

With the coming of the adolescent period of adjustment there is greater need than ever for consideration of the *individual* child. Personality traits are not uniform in childhood, but in the crucial years of change the differentiation becomes more marked. Less and less can they be dealt with according to mere chronological age. The increasing maturity must not lead shortsighted church-school superintendents to conclude that graded lessons are no longer necessary and one uniform lesson can be "applied" to all. Rather, as the interests diverge, more diversified materials are called for. This is real "personal work."

In junior high school the pupil is beginning the study of history in contrast to mere historical anecdote. Is it not true also that among his life needs is a knowledge of the history of the religious tradition which he inherits along with the history of his own country? American history is not taught for the purpose of giving edifying moral truths in each lesson, though misguided patriots do often defend tendential perversions for national glorification. History is taught for the value that lies in the knowledge of its truth. Simplification ought not to mean falsification; the spirit of investigation, not the spirit of propaganda, should rule.

When we apply this to religious history, it is easier to describe the ideal than to provide the materials for carrying it out. Obviously, the third chapter of this book could not be profitably used with fourteen-year-old children. Some of the historical issues discussed there are too complex for comprehension or fruitful use at such an age. To write a true and graphic account is beset with great difficulties as is witnessed in the attempts by able men to fulfill this great need. Probably the most adequate is the text in the Abingdon Weekday Series. Many New Testament scholars are almost unfitted by their very specialization in the field, while professional religious educators appear often to be such zealous devotees of "method" that they are unwilling to let history tell its own story.

The attention of religious educators has been focused upon the preparation of texts which seek to lead young people to a Christian solution of their life problems. Little attempt is made in these to recover the historical context of the biblical passage except as it may show the relation to the modern problem. Rather, the question is put, "What does Jesus expect of young people to-day?" That is the title of a little series of questions that has much to commend it, provoking thought upon the perplexing problems of youth. We have had a large number of discussion outlines to stimulate discovery through Jesus of a Christian way of life. The attempt is made to interpret his ideals in terms of modern life.

Of the necessity of achieving this objective and its fundamental place in any curriculum, there can be not the slightest doubt. The question is, rather, concerning the effectiveness of the procedures now followed and the dangers involved therein. Are we justified in forsaking entirely with youth all avowedly historical study of Jesus? Can we study him fruitfully through the approach of our present problems? One of the keenest leaders of the religious education movement has aptly expressed the indictment against this procedure. "He [Jesus] was unmarried and at the crucial period of his life he lived outside of the family; apparently he had no settled place of abode, and it is not clear that he made any economic contribution to his own support. In short, he did not have our particular problems to meet, and to imitate his conduct is no solution of them."[2]

It should be unnecessary to elaborate upon this after our consideration of the historical mission of Jesus. Our pupils know little about him; many of the current courses make no endeavor to remedy this ignorance. But through the waving of a magician's wand, it is assumed, for instance, that a solution of the race problem will emerge by citing the contact of Jesus with the Samaritans. It is very unlikely that the verse, "Go not into the way of the Samaritans," will also be brought to their attention. But when all the evidence is in, it will lead only to disappointment to cherish the expectation that any series of passages will afford us specific guidance. It is in the casuistry of the application of "principles" that our real problems lie.

For example, when a puzzling race issue arose in the meeting of the college Conference on Religion in a Detroit hotel in December, 1930, there were many earnest young people who sought for the solution of the problem from Jesus, as they had been taught by current Bible study methods. Quite naturally, the advocates of both solutions could support their opinions by quoting proof-text situations from the Gospels. When it was finally realized that there was no way out of the dilemma in this fashion, not a few raised the query, "Of what use is this 'Jesus way of life'

---

[2] Coe, G. A., *What Is Christian Education?* P. 31. Charles Scribner's Sons. This and the following quotations used by special permission.

if it fails to give us guidance in a real emergency?" The answer had been given, as a matter of fact, by the man who gave the keynote address of that Conference: "The literary treasures of the Bible can make a great contribution to the taste side of character. The least important function of the Scriptures is their contribution of dependable, critically sifted data for the solution of our problems. ... The Bible is not a book of solutions."[3]

We would criticize the great majority of these discussion courses on the ground that they are not consequent enough. They have been a necessary transition stage in the development of Christian education. They have made inevitable concessions to the expectations and prejudices of the educational leadership of the local churches. "The Christian religion can employ problem-project teaching consistently and effectively only to the extent that Christianity itself is a problem and an unfinished task."[4] Until that point of view is reached, we will continue to dishonor Jesus as a problem-solver who yet leaves us in the lurch at our most crucial moments. The only way to solve our problems is to study *them* in the light of all the facts that bear upon them.

Two Types of Courses

Hence we plead for a frank twofold division of courses when pupils come to the age when they can think objectively and historically. Much of our study, possibly most, should be focused about the contemporary problems of life. We will seek earnestly for the "mind of Christ" upon them, but we will not expect that there is any book

[3] Coe, G. A., *op. cit.*, p. 194.
[4] *Op. cit.*, p. 189.

that can be opened to present this to us. Diligent thinking and painful experimentation are the roads we must travel. This is the only way to follow the creative example of Jesus. The solutions we so earnestly seek must come from a consideration of the facts themselves by the enlightened conscience.

But how is the mind of Christ to be attained? Not by distilling abstract "principles" or "ideals" to be "applied" in totally different situations. We do not see how the "mind of Christ" can be appreciated apart from a historical study of the actual Jesus of Nazareth, who he was and what he tried to do. It is not difficult to understand why some religious educators prefer to avoid such a procedure. Less opposition from traditionalists can be expected even in a discussion of Jesus on war and race than in a frank presentation of the historical mission of Jesus.

The results of the biblical criticism of the New Testament have not yet been absorbed even by the mass of the ministry, much less by the lay membership of the church. We do not accuse religious educators of "trimming." We do believe that many of them have failed to see the absolute necessity for an energetic grappling with the dissemination of changed points of view. They doubtless say to themselves that as long as there is so much difference of opinion among scholars and uncertainty concerning results, it would be better to pass such questions by. They are not as vital as getting a Christian viewpoint on the great issues of our time. These practical considerations contain much truth. But if we really do believe that Jesus still matters, it ought to be of primary significance to know him truly. Because we must face in all candidness the Christianization of our life, we would plead at the same time for an untrammeled utilization of project and discussion methods. We want to see both points of view utilized, but without the dilution or compromise that comes from a combination.

Place for the two types of courses ought to be found if we really unify the educational program of the church. Correlation of the work of the young people's societies with that of the church school moves forward, though very slowly in many local churches. But can two hours of discussion be fruitful without the devotion of some time to the acquiring of factual information? We must wait a long time for truth to emerge from the exchange of ignorant prejudices. Concerning the factual information that must underlie any solution of such problems as are involved in war, industry, race, sex, there is no occasion here to speak. There must be opportunity, however, for acquiring these facts that may in themselves lack immediate interest. So it is with knowledge of the Bible. Difference of opinion will persist as to what knowledge is fruitful. Just how much of the history of Israel is it advisable that all Christians know? But we cannot see how there can be wide difference of opinion of the importance of what Jesus said and did. If we are to plan two sessions for young people on Sunday, it would seem that at least twice during the ages from thirteen to twenty-one it would serve the needs of youth systematically to undertake such a study.

In the appended bibliography some of the better textbook materials have been listed. However, we must confess that there is no one volume that can be unreservedly commended. Where it is possible, the teacher should use for himself the best historical manuals available and lead his students in a study of the Gospels themselves. While readable lives of Jesus can be of great help, nothing can take the place of the study of the sources which are actually in the hands of everyone. One resourceful teacher of high-school girls organized a project in her class—the writing of a life of Christ to be sent to a school in Japan. The girl with the best account for the day could have hers incorporated in the book they were making. We must never confuse a project which we set with one which rises spontaneously from the experience of the class. Nevertheless, such a procedure may suggest how increased interest may be cultivated.

After all, the interest of the class will be determined very much by the enthusiasm of the teacher. High-school students embark upon many subjects for which they have no preliminary eagerness. The result usually depends upon the ability of the teacher to make it vivid and living. We will not awaken interest in Jesus if our information is bounded by the manual we are teaching. It will not be stimulated by accepting every possible excuse to wander off upon "topics of the day." It is a damaging confession that we really do not believe Jesus to be important. Such digressions will not be necessary if their subjects are made the object of definite, planned study at other times.

The separation for which we are pleading will make possible the truer presentation of the "fourfold life." This popular description of the Christian ideal has much to commend it. But the brief summary from Luke 2. 52 does not suffice to show that the life of Jesus was what we would call "well-rounded." As a matter of fact, he cultivated neither intellectual nor cultural interests but devoted himself one-sidedly to his religious mission. We always need some one-sided geniuses, but for the average person, fullness of life should mean a "fourfold life" with physical and mental, social and spiritual development.

THE STUDY OF BOOKS

Despite the spread of graded materials in the church schools, it is still probably true that the majority of classes for older pupils use the international improved uniform lessons. In recent years the custom has been adopted of following through one individual Gospel. Hence Luke is studied for one six-month period; John during another, and Matthew during another. This method has obvious advantages and equal disadvantages. Difficult historical questions may be passed by when we set for ourselves the task of studying a book just as it stands. It will depend upon the individual teacher whether there is to be a real grappling with the Jesus of history, or whether the printed passage is simply to be taken as the text for a sermon, or the point of departure for the consideration of some modern problem. There is value in studying one consecutive account, for each Gospel has its own character. Though the synoptic Gospels draw upon common bodies of tradition each evangelist has stamped his story with his own personality.

The method, however, has the disadvantage of setting neither a historical question nor a modern problem. We really seek to know not Matthew nor Luke, but Jesus. Luke's account of the story is invaluable, but we cannot stop there. We must compare and contrast if we are to recover the Jesus of history. Nor does the study of a book provide a free and favorable setting for the study of our modern problems. The procedure may be studied at its best in Bruce Curry's *Jesus and His Cause*. Mark is divided into fifteen sections which are more or less unified under single themes. After a consideration of these various "periods" in the life of Jesus, the individual problem is isolated for discussion in its contemporary aspects. This "book study" plan makes possible a very much more historical treatment than the average problem course on the life and teachings of Jesus. But we wonder if the objectives could not better be attained separately pursued.

THE ULTIMATE PROBLEM OF LIFE

The fascinating and difficult attempt to discover a Christian solution to the problems of war, race, industry, the family and a young man's lifework, cannot be discussed within the limits of this book. That does not mean that Jesus has nothing to say to us upon them. It should be impossible to study him with any care and not become more acutely aware of the pagan aspects of our civilization. The ideals of his life will offer significant guidance in our judgment of values. We will discover what we can do next about them, however, only as we conscientiously face the facts of the world as it is. It would take a whole book to discuss any one of these problems. We ought not to lead students to expect that it is within the province of religion to furnish ready-made decisions. Jesus will be a ferment touching our thinking upon them at ever new and unexpected places.

Beside these pressing problems it may appear irrelevant to some modern men and women to discuss the problem

of the virgin birth, the resurrection, and such questions
that do perplex young and old about religion. Though
they are not major in themselves, they often stand in the
way of a fruitful relation of our lives to Jesus. The
teacher who can help his pupils at such points will do an
inestimable service. We desire here to call attention to
the excellent treatment in Miss Streibert's *Youth and the
Bible*. Some teachers will feel that they have not themselves made up their minds on certain of the questions
relating to Jesus. Instead of avoiding difficult discussion,
it is much better to state clearly the different positions
so that the pupils may think along with the teacher upon
the problem. Doubt is not uncertainty about facts;
doubt has given up the religious quest, and has settled
back into an accepted rejection of religious faith. Such
doubt does not come from honest uncertainty, but from
disillusionment with blind dogmatism.

We are apt to forget that behind all of the immediate
and pressing problems that perplex youth lies the ultimate
problem of God. Not that its philosophical or theological
aspects bear upon their immediate experience. Their
belief in God must be practical, not theoretical. The
God of Whitehead and Lloyd Morgan will never have
influence beyond university circles. The God of Jesus
was a living Person that completely controlled the
career of his challenging life. The patterns of science
will furnish to us the most fruitful analogies for our
thought about God. But it takes the life of a man like
Jesus to stimulate our faith in the *reality* of any real God.

It is not a vague, mystical concept that our pupils need.
They are not likely to respond to the account of one who
paid the price for us in some suprahistorical transaction.

A heavenly Being who condescended to come down to earth to dwell will have few points of contact with their experience. Amid all the pleas for more religious education for our youth we must never forget that it is supremely important *what* is taught. Jesus must fit into the total world of reality that maturing experience builds up. We must see him as he was.

What is there in the life and teachings of Jesus that can contribute directly to the development of life during adolescent and mature years? What are the values that emerge from a study of the historical Jesus? To that question we will turn in the succeeding chapter. But one preliminary objection should be noted. How can anyone truthfully claim that the study of Jesus will be so fruitful as is asserted? Has he really been a transforming power to those who have studied him? Is there any justifiable reason to expect that the Jesus of modern historical scholarship will be so much more potent than the sacramental and theological and mystical Christs that have been the center of so much teaching in the past? Can the "dynamic of Jesus" be demonstrated in actual practice? We believe that it can. Sure and invariable results, however, cannot be expected from any kind of religious teaching. We hope to improve our techniques of presenting him, though past failures should warn us against claiming certain and automatic results. Jesus will offer dynamic to life only as men respond to his appeal. There are those who will remain cold to the values we find in Jesus. If any other influence brings inspiration to them, we can only rejoice. But those who have found in him their highest inspiration will continue striving to present him more adequately and compellingly.

CHAPTER VI

MODERN VALUES IN JESUS

"What lessons may I draw from the life of Jesus?"
How often is such a question put! It is not only the
scholar who in his minute study pulverizes the portrait
into pieces. According to current methods of religious
teaching, we take fifteen verses of the record from which
to draw "lessons"; or, we go for a word or incident con-
tributing to the solution of our problem. We do not
apply often enough the "lesson" of the life of Jesus in its
totality. We need a vision of the whole brought to a
focus so that the mind can grasp its meaning. Eloquent
tributes to Jesus we have in abundance drawn from the
anthologies of religious literature. Too often they are
meaningless because they are not linked with reality.
Yet countless Christians do not have a total picture of
what Jesus actually tried to do.

Some of our newer manuals are trying to introduce
even the younger student to the study of Jesus by a brief
picture of the whole story. One of our progressive
thinkers in religious education recounts his experience in
a worship service in a boys' camp, the climax of a week's
series conducted as a controlled experiment. We quote
from his report:

"The final service, which brought the conference to a
close, was centered about a realistic story of the life of
Jesus. The story, from the birth at Nazareth to the crucifixion in Jerusalem and the later activity of the disciples,

was told within the space of about thirty minutes. Endeavor was made to include only those events which would be generally agreed upon as historically supported. No stress was laid upon the items which had been omitted, but the skeleton of known truth was put in a vivid, dramatic form. The attempt was made to let the purposes, choices, and events of the extraordinarily thrilling life of Jesus speak for themselves."[1]

It is no surprise to learn that upon almost every count this service was ranked as the most effective in the series. But students will never gain the impression of "an extraordinarily thrilling life" if it is broken up into prosaic "lessons."

The "whole" is significant because its "parts" likewise have value for us. We must be ready, however, to meet the contention that this cannot be the case, since Jesus belongs to the long ago. It is easy for superficial young people to look down on one who never rode in an auto, nor saw an aeroplane, nor even heard of radio. But the wisdom of life stands in no relation to such things. There are realms where the latest supersedes all that has gone before. Science and technology move forward on relatively straight lines. Not so, however, with the wisdom of the ages. It is understood only by him who has ears to hear. In the appreciation of ultimate insights we do not begin where the last generation left off. We must start anew, if not from "scratch," at least far from the goals already attained.

The temporary elements that appear in the study of Jesus call for no apology on our part, for there is no

---

[1] Watson, G. B., "An Approach to the Study of Worship," in *Religious Education*, vol. xxiv, pp. 853f. Used by special permission.

possible timeless expression of ideas. If there are imper-
manent elements in the Gospels, they are likewise to be
found at every other point in history. The most modern
fashions in thought will doubtless prove the most temporary of all. Since the permanent message of any man
must be expressed in the thought of some one age, it
makes relatively little difference that Jesus lived two
thousand years ago rather than two hundred. Allowance
will have to be made in the year 2000 for the purely
contemporary elements in any message which we believe
we have for posterity.

Jesus leaps in a unique way over the changing centuries
because he spoke to unchanging needs of the heart of man.
Theologies are soon outgrown, for they are attempts in a
contemporary thought mold to systematize the data of
religious experience. The experiences themselves have
more abiding significance. The Indian Upanishads become the basis for a chapter in the history of Oriental
philosophy, but the Vedic hymns reach elemental depths
of common experience. So Jesus speaks to us, not as an
antiquated first-century theologian, but as one who knew
what was in the heart of man. He expounded no doc-
trines but lived great life convictions, and hence speaks
to the living experience of all time.

One of the great words of the fourth Gospel sums up
most of what Jesus means to us. "I came that they may
have life, and may have *it* abundantly."[2] The great
value of the fourth Gospel is that it gives explicit statement to that which was only implicit in the earlier records.
It puts upon the lips of Jesus the convictions which men
had come to entertain after two generations of Christian

[2] John 10. 10.

fellowship. The content and nature of that "life" are set forth in the Gospel of John in terms which William James would have described as decidedly "thin." It must be filled with "thickness" from the more historical records of the synoptic Gospels. But no other word gives a more adequate expression to what men have found in Jesus. We will divide the description of this life under eight main headings, and endeavor to see how these relate themselves to the needs of modern young people and adults.

GOOD HEALTH

This life meant, first of all, *good health*. No argument is necessary to show that this commands the interest of all of us. The war against disease is being waged along a long battle front. "Success" means little if one does not retain the health to enjoy it. Our ludicrous fads and pathetic eagerness to test the promises for patent medicines show how widespread is the quest for health. Pulsating life must have a physical foundation.

Jesus did not occupy himself with the saving of "souls," as do some latter-day evangelists. The word translated "soul" in Mark 8. 35 in the Authorized Version is more correctly rendered "life" in the Revised Version. Jesus did not consider souls apart from bodies but thought of life as a whole. The Gospels recount very few stories of what we would call *conversions*.[3] Healing incidents however abound. There is no indication that Jesus sought to avoid a ministry to the bodies of men. When he is reported as saying, "Let us go elsewhere into the next towns, that I may preach there also," the contrast

---

[3] Only Luke 19. 1-10 and possibly 7. 35ff. in the synoptic Gospels.

is not between preaching and healing, but between the one village and the others that should not only hear his good tidings, but likewise enjoy sounder health.

One reason for the interest of Jesus in better health does not apply in the modern situation. We do not believe that sickness is a divine punishment for sin, as did many first-century Jews. Only once does the question arise in the gospel narratives of the forgiveness of sin as a prerequisite for the healing.[4] That Jesus rejected the dogma that misfortunes were a punishment for sin seems clear from a comment on certain well-known contemporary catastrophes. If it were true that the tower of Siloam fell upon eighteen unfortunates because of their sin, what saved the self-righteous questioners from a similar doom?[5] Since Jesus depended not upon magic but the awakening of faith for his healing ministry, it is altogether probable that an assurance of divine forgiveness sometimes accompanied his appeal for faith.

Occasionally Jesus is reported as having used popular methods of healing, but usually it was by the word.[6] Which accounts are legendary and which have a basis in fact we cannot determine in detail, but there is no denying that he exercised an important healing mission. For Jesus it had transcendent importance. Especially what were looked on then as demon exorcisms evidenced the overthrow of Satan and the collapse of his power.[7] Good health was an integral part of the life he came to bring.

We carry on his work as we labor earnestly for the

[4] Mark 2. 1-10.
[5] Luke 13. 4.
[6] Except Mark 8. 22-26; 7. 31-37.
[7] Matthew 11. 2-6; 12. 27-28; Luke 13. 32.

improvement of public health. Because scientific medicine was unknown to him, we are not warranted in neglecting its aid. The cures which he was able to effect will be a permanent reminder that man is more than a physical organism, and that drugs will not suffice to heal all of his diseases. We will not set arbitrary bounds to the power of faith, nor will we, on the other hand, call any less divine the healing that utilizes surgical skill or scientifically tested drugs.

It is a mistake, however, to talk about "athletes of the Bible," or to assume that Jesus would have been interested in football. The cultivation of either the body or the mind for its own sake did not challenge his interest. For good or for ill, his work was exclusively religious. Many of our texts for boys to the contrary, it cannot be said that Jesus' life was well rounded. Jesus gave himself completely to *one* thing. If a completely rounded life is our aim, we will neither further it nor honor Jesus by making claims which are not borne out by the records. Whether as an eagle scout or a captain of industry, modern categories simply do not fit the Man of Galilee. In so far as these interests are legitimate they can assuredly stand on their own feet. He burned out his own life in the quest of an ideal beside which his own health was quite secondary. We too should discover that health is but a means of realizing other higher values. This introduces a further emphasis in Jesus.

THE PRIMACY OF SPIRITUAL VALUES

To keep first things first is an aim of all successful living. What scale of values will determine our choices and govern the ends we seek? How can we discover the really worth-while things in life? These questions face everyone anew. We may adopt a hypothesis, but life itself must answer the question.

It is unfortunately misleading to talk about the primacy of spiritual values, for "spiritual" is one of those words that defies exact definition. That health and wealth both have spiritual potentialities ought to be abundantly clear. But we must recognize that Jesus believed that the abundant life did not consist in the multitude of *material possessions*. He believed that they choked life, the life of him who possessed them, and of him who did not. It is a gross anachronism to classify Jesus as a Socialist. He sought more wealth for no one, and warned all of its perils. It was possible to write with some plausibility of the "Call of the Carpenter," but no one could recognize Jesus under the "Call of the Capitalist." Possessions were to him not an opportunity but a peril. His own wandering life cannot be made a model for a continuing society, but it is a permanent challenge to the gospel of comfort and ease which creeps in so insidiously to harbor the germs of decay and degeneration.

The kingdom of God, no matter how we reinterpret it, cannot be made into a matter of colored-tile bathrooms for all. Jesus called men not to greater luxury but to uncompromising loyalty to a transcendent religious goal. One captivated with the ideals of bigness, and heaping gold reserves, billions of machine horse power, and mass production of standardized goods cannot be expected to respond to the real Jesus until he finds in him a "transvaluation of all values." His values are quite incommensurable with those dealt with on Wall Street, and those believed in on most of the country estates of Long Island.

Many interpreters of Jesus discover in his words a teaching of the doctrine of stewardship.[8] That he believed life to be a trust from God is evident. That he gave any guidance on a Christian way to make money, or invest money, or spend money is not so clear. The young people of our generation face an unsolved problem in discovering how to make a living and a life at the same time, without being enslaved by Mammon. The problem has a different aspect for every separate individual. What Jesus does is to present every one of us with an inescapable challenge to standards of materialism.

We must never imagine, however, that Jesus stood for an *ascetic* attitude toward life. If there were those who had made themselves eunuchs for the sake of the Kingdom, they had sacrificed genuine goods in the supreme cause.[9] Deprivation for its own sake was never exalted. Jesus never sought to cramp life. We have called attention previously to the significant instructions whereby his followers were to travel light for efficiency sake, but there was no credit in going without essentials. The long, painful story of self-mutilation and flagellation in the name of religion finds no basis in Jesus. The spiritual had a healthy basis in the material. Sacrifice was always in the interest of the larger good.

SINCERITY

Our assumed scale of values presents a test to the *sincerity* of our religion. It is a test whereby much contemporary religion has been held to be found wanting. Professions and practice do not agree, we are often re-

---

[8] As in Luke 16. 11; 19. 11-28.
[9] Matthew 19. 12.

minded. The high-sounding phrases we use are mean-ingless, say the skeptics of religion. The real values which a man cherishes are not those to which he pays eloquent tribute but those which really control his con-duct. Here many religious people do not show themselves more spiritually minded than their contemporaries who do without the luxury of these high professions.

We cannot stop for an exact analysis of the truth in such charges, but the religious teacher should permit no such easy generalities to pass unexamined. We want here to see the appeal for absolute sincerity which lay in Jesus. The life that he exalted was not for dilettantes. He was the persistent foe of all "posing" in religion. All special activities of religion were fraught with this peril. Alms-giving was not discouraged, but it must be divorced from every suspicion of ostentation. Since the only merit in fasting lay in the humiliation of the heart before God, any outward signs would introduce the subtle temptation to advertise our piety. Even public prayers came in for criticism on the same ground, though we should never forget that the publican whose prayer was accepted in the beautiful parable-example in Luke 18 uttered his petition in a most public place. To reduce such words of Jesus to legislation would simply redouble the dangers of insincerity.

In the extreme inwardness of the morality of the Sermon on the Mount, we have one extended description of the sincere life. Hatred is equivalent to murder and lust to adultery, for, measured by the rod of sincerity, these are the final outcomes of the genuine desires. Legal statutes are only concerned with actual wrongs suffered. Jesus was thinking of the individual whose quality of life was determined by his inmost desires. A good tree brings forth only good fruit, but we cannot argue from respectable deeds to a good man. Only that which springs from a genuine heart of good will is really good.

In the realm of speech sincerity always finds important applications. The words from Jesus about the use of oaths do not apply primarily to the coarse and disgusting habit of profanity. That will, of course, have its place in the discussions of a class in religion. It is pathetic when people attempt to enlarge a poverty-stricken vocabulary by the addition of oaths, and end by reducing their speech to these formulas. Of course, as all other Jews of his time, Jesus believed that the name of God was so holy that it should hardly be uttered at all. But what he had in mind in his attack upon oaths was the current practice, among even the pious, of using various formulas to strengthen ordinary speech. Some were looked upon as more binding than others.[10] Jesus would cut through all of this casuistry of speech with the demand for the simple affirmative or negative. There must be no degrees of truthfulness. He spoke to men who had so watered their ordinary speech by insincerity that it needed strengthening by oaths to carry any conviction. We never hear of Jesus entering upon theoretical debates as to whether occasions may not arise when love demands telling less than the whole truth. Such questions will have to be decided individually. A guiding touch-stone is his unhesitating emphasis upon *sincerity*.

Often we do not say what is in our minds because we know that it has no business to be there. Many of the insincerities of modern life are due to this tension and

---

[10] Matthew 23. 16ff.

division between what we theoretically approve (or more often, society approves), and the dictates of our real desires. A prominent school of thought insists that these conflicts are deleterious, and worse in consequence than the actual expression of our repressed desires. They would find the solution in the removal of the repression. Jesus was no less conscious of the peril of a divided personality. His solution lay rather in giving attention to the "inner eye," to the fountain of the heart.

The sincere and open life is the only one in which there can be a genuine inner peace and satisfaction. It does not always mean outward peace, however. On the contrary, sincerity is seldom welcome where convenient conformity is the most desired goal. And how many spheres of life there are where sincere individual views are held only against intense opposition! If an individual refuses to sacrifice sincerity for conformity, with what spirit shall he meet the opposition that is sure to come? That is a problem that faces everyone in ever new situations. The answer of Jesus is abundantly clear. To apply it and follow it is a less simple matter.

Forgiving Nonretaliation

We have put these two somewhat differing words together because they seem to belong together. The application on a wide scale of nonviolence in India tends to perpetuate the error which Tolstoy made in assuming that nonresistance was the primary teaching of Jesus. As a matter of fact, not the presence or absence of force, but the presence or absence of hatred must be made primary in any interpretation of Jesus. A policy of passive resistance *may* mean nothing more than an absence of any other alternative, while the hearts of men are seething with the hatred which has no opportunity to destroy life.

Basic in the attitude of Jesus was the demand for the forgiving spirit. Social workers to-day do not take much interest in the theological aspects of the "forgiveness of sins." They would call us to work for the eradication of sin, and not encourage a man to rest back in the comfortable faith of the creed, "I believe in the forgiveness of sins." Such a point of view fails to consider that Jesus was primarily interested in the *human* aspect of forgiveness. The belief in the forgiveness of sins that counted with him was the readiness to forgive to "seventy-times-seven," or in other words, that never counted the occasions. True, he grounded this demand upon an ultimate religious basis, "If ye forgive not men their trespasses, neither will your Father forgive your trespasses." But it is clear that the absence of the use of force would not suffice to satisfy the expectation of Jesus.

But what if they do not desire our forgiveness? What if they oppose us with bitter enmity, and for conscience sake? With what weapons is such opposition to be met? Our instinctive inclination is to fight back with kind and return with interest. Every group of young people contains those who sincerely think that any other response is that of a mollycoddle. What was the principle of Jesus, for he assumed that opposition and persecution must be faced if his followers were to be outspoken in their loyalty to him?

His central principle cannot be accurately expressed by "Resist not evil." His whole life was one long resistance to evil. We must not forget that there were swords in the party on the night of the capture of Jesus. It would seem that they were ready to protect themselves against violent assault. If any negative formulation is permissible it is rather "*nonretaliation*." We should not fix our attention primarily upon the hyperbolic illustrations with which Jesus made his teaching vivid. Arguments drawn from absurdity may miss fire when men try to escape undesired conclusions by appeal to an impossible literalism.

Jesus saw the simple alternative, and we must make it clear to our pupils. I may succumb to the poison of another's enmity and return hatred with hatred and opposition with bitter retaliation. Or, I may meet it with *love*, in the hope that ultimately my love may take root in my opponent. There is no guarantee that love will succeed in breaking down evil or misunderstanding. We have no right, however, to expect that anything else will. Such is the boomerang expressed by the old Jewish proverb, "With what measure ye mete, it shall be measured unto you." Nonretaliation is not a resignation of all positive influence, but puts into operation the greatest power of all—self-denying love. Of course it is not the response of the "natural man," but Jesus would insert the prodding question, "What do ye more than others?" Only in the revelation of such love are the sons of the Heavenly Father manifest.[11]

We touch here upon problems of a perplexing and difficult character. Is such an ideal practical for nations or for any groups? We may wrong Jesus here either by too sweeping generalizations, or by soft excuses that would explain it all away. It must not be forgotten that Jesus

[11] Matthew 5. 47-48.

was proposing no amendments to the criminal code of Palestine. The development of a Christian check upon criminality is not to be decided by a text. Christians may decide to take no part in any future war, but they must be willing to take the consequences of their action. These are questions which challenge not only the searching discussion of Christian people, but likewise their conscientious experimentation. Here is a sphere where daring young people may venture some fruitful risks.

If we actually do join in any experiments in the application of love, we are certain to discover what Jesus promised—that it would call for many sacrifices. The cost of Christian discipleship is easy to illustrate from sentences of Jesus. It is not so easy to illustrate in the church life of to-day. In a nominally Christian country the name of Christ bears with it little reproach. So long as we are not prudish or queer most people will respect our religious beliefs. Cross-bearing has degenerated into a euphemism for minor inconveniences and difficulties. The decent respectability which passes in many circles for Christianity is about as dangerous as a poodle dog, and as expensive as dandelions in May. The words of the Gospels will regain their reality only in the extent to which our whole-hearted commitment to the ideals of Jesus actually does bring us into clash with the opposing ideals of a pagan society. When students feel that clash, then it is time to hear the words, "He that loveth father or mother more than me is not worthy of me." And we must likewise hear him say, not retaliation, but love is the weapon with which we must conquer.

This is the heroic demand that Jesus makes to every age. As already noted, his ethic is not ascetic in purpose. It is, rather, a goal toward which heroes will strive. Most of us are not cast in a very heroic mold. That is why the average Christianity of every age has been such a feeble reincarnation of the spirit of Him whom we call Lord. In almost every group of young people there are some possibilities of real moral heroism. Not a "practical" Jesus, but one far ahead of us will appeal to them.

CREATIVE LIVING

Thus far we have been considering an earnest, but possibly somber, ideal. Joy must be a keynote of any abundant life. Our age of intensive mechanization and standardization feels increasingly that some measure of *creative living* is the basis for true happiness. The word itself has been worn threadbare, but we cannot therefore ignore the fact that creative impulses are among the most compelling elements in our nature. What appeal does Jesus make to this side of our being?

The creative principle in Jesus is most readily seen in his relation to the law. We have noted in Chapter III that Jesus accepted in principle the Torah as the divine will of God. To our age of relativity, even in moral standards, Jesus speaks as one who believed that there is an absolute will of God, and not merely the conventions of men. That did not, however, exclude the necessity for creative thinking and acting. Not only did he set aside the "traditions of the elders" on occasion, but his emphatic, "I say unto you," was uttered in contradiction to the explicit statements of the Old Testament. He sought to get behind the letter to the underlying purpose of God. In other words, he brought to bear upon the highest standards of the past his own creative insight.

The Sabbath question will afford a fruitful example to illustrate his method, and one not without modern interest. The written Torah had explicitly forbidden all work. The elaborate prescriptions of the oral traditions, which amuse twentieth-century scoffers, had arisen to mitigate the stringency of this prohibition. According to the consensus of the rabbis, it was permitted to save life on the Sabbath, but Jesus did not stop at healings in cases where there was immediate danger. Since the day had been instituted of God for the benefit of man, it could not be wrong to do good on the Sabbath. It is an instructive witness to the effect of the example of Jesus that there is no evidence in the New Testament that the observance of the Jewish Sabbath (as a day when it was sinful to do any work) was enjoined upon Gentile Christians. Nor is there any evidence in the first century that its provisions were transferred to the Lord's Day. Though the Puritan is little more than a memory in most communities, not a few bad consciences remain amid the "loosening of standards." It is a shame that zealous religionists have often been lined up against Jesus on this point. Like the Pharisees of old, they have been more intent upon defending a day than providing for the God-given needs of men. We cannot study the Sabbath question in the Gospels without striving for a more creative attitude for our own day. When our finest young people speak out their real minds, it will be as shocking to some of their elders as was the conduct of Jesus.

It would not serve the objective of this chapter to rehearse the full story of Jesus' critical and constructive attitude toward the law. We do not lead creative lives by any process of mere imitation of his conduct in the few spheres where we have analogous accounts. The importance of Jesus does not lie in affording us a rule of thumb to follow. Whatever the "Jesus way of life" may mean, it does not mean tracing a given blue print. As a matter of fact, that current phrase is not a very happy description of the significance of Jesus. The Judaism of his time presented to men a most explicit "way of life," and to this day that is what Judaism has been. It has offered the widest latitude in belief, but definite prescription in rules of conduct, and has surrounded these with religious sanctions. A much more liberal and indefinite connotation is given to the "Christian way of life"; but we miss the leadership of Jesus if we overlook the fact that it is first, last, and always a way of progress. The way of Jesus does not even lie in following a set group of principles. It consists in *bringing to the highest insight of the past, devout criticism and fertile thinking*. The fuller will of God is yet to be discovered, and Jesus would trust the open mind to find it. The legacy of Jesus did not include a detailed map of the kingdom of God. Following him is following the spirit of truth in this adventurous pursuit of the good life.

Here is the basis for the so-called project principle in religious education. We do not make it Christian by the number of citations to gospel passages for help in the "solution" of our problems. We make it Christian by the honesty with which we face the facts which painstaking research reveals, and the respect for persons that motivates our resultant choices. From such an education there is some hope of creating a new world. Jesus challenges us to follow him in creative living.

We noted in Chapter III that Jesus seemed to make

respect for personality the central principle in his attitude toward the law. That requires one qualification, however. Jesus was not anthropocentric in his viewpoint. God was the center of his life. The will of the Father was supreme with him. Humanitarianism is no adequate description of his religion. Respect for personality had significance because men were children of God. It was a clue to the will of God, not simply to finer social relations. This theocentric point of view is frankly alien to many of our generation. God is very doubtful to them; social values are the only certain goods. To talk about the "will of God," to their mind, only gives unwarranted and dangerous prestige to certain particular patterns in the changing social world.

It is frankly the parting of the ways between Jesus with his truly humane spirit, and that orphaned humanism which finds no evidence of cosmic support for its ideals. The way of high religion must do without God, according to some modern interpreters.[12] If so, they must leave Jesus out of the catalogue of its exponents, for God was the center of his life. Those who follow him see just as clearly the peril of an imperfectly moralized God. They will tolerate no sanctification of any *status quo* under the assumption that it represents the divine will. There is no sphere of life where we have a right to assume that experimentation will not reveal finer social possibilities. But the true creator will, like Jesus, appreciate the values in the past, and he will believe that the new is valid, not because it is new, but because it corresponds to reality. In other words, it is a closer approximation of the will of God under the given conditions.

---

[12] Lippmann, Walter, *A Preface to Morals.*

HUMBLE SERVICE

Truly creative living may remain a flying objective for most of us. But what are the guiding attitudes that shall govern us? What fundamental qualities of life should mark the genuine Christian? We have already named sincerity, and would now add *humility* and *service*. The creative ideal of some of our contemporaries leads to self-sufficiency and to independence. Its mood is reflected in the slogan, "I am the Master of my fate." Humility is not a virtue in a pagan, secular society. Certainly it is not a dominant Anglo-Saxon characteristic. The blessings upon the meek and the poor in spirit are not taken as seriously as the rewards that appear to come to the pushing and self-confident.

The humility that Jesus would cultivate must not be made to exclude that sound self-love which he recognized as the basis of all human relations. "Thou shalt love thy neighbor as thyself." But we must give the same high evaluation to all of the other sons of God. As one of our great preachers has stated it, "Humility is not thinking meanly of yourself; it is not thinking of yourself at all." It is the antithesis of self-consciousness. It is not an obsequious bowing before other men, but a reverence before the Shaper of destinies, who "taketh up the isles as a very little thing.'

We may discuss the nature of humility in our class and the specious substitutes which walk in its disguise. We may point out the self-defeating character of bumptious self-assertion. But on the whole these are attitudes of character too subtle for direct preaching of any kind. It is in our services of worship that skillful variations must be played upon this chord, touching the springs of the emotional life. Humility is our response to the infinite and eternal. It should be our attitude toward our fellow men, for in the lowest of these there is still something of these divine qualities.

There follows naturally the obligation *to serve*. Instead of quoting once more the well-known texts illustrating Jesus' practice and precept in this regard, it would be well to face the fact that "service" is a word which has lost its effectiveness for our generation. Pious admonitions to service simply fall upon deaf ears. It is instructive to notice, therefore, that we have general words from Jesus only in connection with the principle that the great man is the servant, not the one who lords it over others. Elsewhere we always find concrete descriptions of specific things done to help others,[13] or examples which he himself set in his own life.[14]

Here is a place where we can learn from the pedagogy of Jesus. Instead of *talking* about service, we can plan definite tasks that need to be done, and the best ways of getting them accomplished. One class "talk-fest" could well be omitted while the members were out doing something that they had decided ought to be done. The discovery of these needs will call for the creative spirit of which we have spoken. If Jesus were telling the parable of the good Samaritan to a modern audience, the details would be quite different. But the challenge to any religion that neglects practical neighborliness abides unchanged. Not everyone that saith unto me, "Service! Service!" but he that *doeth*.

---

[13] Luke 10. 30ff.; Matthew 25. 35ff.
[14] Luke 22. 27; John 13. 1-11.

LIFE RECEIVED

These active elements in the religion of Jesus call forth the readiest response in most of our young people. To the exuberance of their youth religion must present something for them to do. There are others to whom the meditative and receptive aspects are just as appealing. This will not be the case with all, and we cannot force appreciations before they are genuine. Maturer experience will realize most clearly why Jesus believed that abundant life was ultimately a gift of God. His greatest apostle wrote, "What hast thou that thou didst not receive?" In three ways we may distinguish how Jesus thought that life was received.

(1) Life was received in *prayer*. Jesus did not speculate about the problem of prayer, but at every crisis of his life we find him turning naturally and inevitably to the Father. So impressed were the disciples by the resources from his prayer life that they took the initiative in asking how to pray. The few brief recorded prayers of the Master are among the most treasured gems of the gospel tradition. The treatment of the prayer life of Jesus in Deissmann's *The Religion of Jesus and the Faith of Paul* would be found rewarding by every teacher.

Many honest teachers will face difficulty in some of the teaching about prayer ascribed to him. We may not find it easy to think of God in as personal a way as did Jesus. Inheriting a belief in the orderly processes of a world of law, we may candidly look upon some of the words as incredible. Wonderful sentiments about prayer will not grip us if the sense of reality be lacking.

At the heart of the difficulty lie two little stories of

Jesus enforcing persistence in prayer.[15]   Jesus seems to say that if an unrighteous judge will redress the wrongs of a widow who nags continuously, and if a comfort-loving householder will yet arise to give bread to an embarrassed neighbor, how much more will God answer the requests of those who cry to him.   The not unnatural interpretation is that Jesus means to urge upon men persistence in claiming their own desires at the throne of heaven.

Such was not the attitude of Jesus himself, however, at the most crucial hour of his life.   Another comparison would likewise give us pause.   If a son ask of his father bread, he will not give him a stone, but it does not follow that he will give him anything that he desires.   The nature of the good gifts will be controlled by the more mature wisdom of the parent.   Hence we are tempted to return to the words recalled in the preceding paragraph and see if they will bear another interpretation.

A discriminating distinction has been made between a Sultanic view of prayer and a scientific.   The former draws its analogy from the Oriental court, where the will of the petitioner may be wheedled out of the monarch by a close study of his weaknesses, the observance of proper formulas, and the utilization of favorite intermediaries. The latter turns for its model to the procedure of the scientist, who persistently puts his leading questions to nature, not expecting to tease his will out of the universe, but believing that patient persistence will lead to understanding. Scientific research continually verifies the promise, "For everyone that asketh receiveth; and he that seeketh findeth; and to him that knocketh it shall be opened."

[15] Luke 11. 5-8; 18. 1-8.

Are we wrong in believing that Jesus had something similar in mind when he sought by vivid illustration to enforce the truth that Heaven's ears were closed to the easy oral petition? Since he suffered no inhibitions from ideas of natural law, it may be going too far to attribute such modern ideas to him. It may suggest the kind of response his example may awaken in us. Only the prayer of "dominant desire" can find an answer. But he who prays earnestly will discover that life is given. We must learn how to receive through this channel.

(2) Life was received in free *forgiveness*. Jesus completely rejected the idea that anyone could earn a reward from God. Our duty is never done. Anyone who has taken seriously the expectations set forth in the Sermon on the Mount can never consider himself righteous, no matter how he may appear beside his fellow men. Anyone who has learned from Jesus what the way of life should be is doomed to a sense of failure and defeat. Well may his earnest followers ask to-day, "Where are the Christians?" Judged by his standard, there are none. What response can we find to this realization of sin?

Though few modern young people brood over their sins, they cannot help but be interested in a new chance. To receive that, is to receive new life. That happened when men met Jesus. Though it was no new discovery for a Jew that God was merciful and forgiving, men believed it then with a certainty that was new. After his death forgiveness of sins was proclaimed in the name of Jesus, and to historic Christianity it has been the most precious boon of our religion.

Divorced from the radical, ethical imperatives of Jesus, this emphasis has sometimes resulted in a religion which cultivated inner states of feeling rather than vital, ethical transformation of character. That is no final reason why we should belittle this element in the *life* that Jesus expected men to receive from the hand of God. We cannot afford to lose this sense of acceptance by God, even though we fall short of his expectations. There is no abundant life without the ever-present hope of new beginnings, even amid failure and defeat.

(3) Life must be received because only God can send his kingdom. As we have seen, it was not to be built by human hands. Though man could prepare for its coming, only God could usher in the time when his will would be done on earth as it was in heaven. There was no self-salvation in the thought of Jesus. Neither did he think of individuals being carried away to heaven. The redeemed life was social; men must become the kind of individuals who could participate in a new order of society. Though he expected its arrival in a manner that did not take place and which it is impossible for us to hold to-day, the essential truth still abides. Every individual must prepare to take part in a new order of society. To call our labors on behalf of prohibition, or government ownership of basic industries, or social settlements, "work for the kingdom of God" is a very doubtful extension of terminology. It is an assumption of omniscience on our part, and begs the question in advance. Only experiment and discovery will demonstrate what "reforms" bring more good than ill. No one of us can sufficiently overcome personal bias to state infallibly that the benefits are more than to one particular group. We will continue earnestly all our efforts for a better social order, but with great modesty in claiming divine approval for our opinions.

More important is the preservation of the original belief that God would send his kingdom. A kingdom of God can come only in so far as its ideals fit into the universe as it really is. No kingdom of God can be built in a world that is ultimately hostile to its principles of love. Many believe to-day that this is the case. Some, with curious inconsistency, reject all belief in God, for they think that such a belief makes struggle unreal, guaranteeing the goal in advance. Others profess belief in a God of personal salvation, but are at the same time very certain that the ideals of Jesus can have no possible place in the world of reality, business, politics, and industry. As opposed to both, lies the essence of the faith of Jesus. Our only hope in the realization of that more ideal world that we call "the kingdom of God" lies in the extent to which the universe is friendly to its coming. Without God, it is not possible. "With God, all things are possible." Unless there are such resources in the universe, all of our struggles will bring us only futile exercise and endless disappointment. Naturally, we think of the relation of God to the world in very different terms than any first-century Jew. How we may utilize all our available resources must be discovered by pioneers of the human spirit. But we can never get beyond the basic faith of Jesus that God must send his kingdom.

Enervating quietism will be avoided if the teacher never fails to come back to the truth, "God must send it *through you.*" All that we do may be human and inadequate, but that is no excuse for doing nothing. However, we do easily falter and fail. Quickly do we grow weary in well-doing. We lack the moral courage and spiritual inspiration to stick to our hard tasks during the long periods when everything seems to be against us. Do our students have a fair-weather religion, expecting to receive the victory at once, or have they the power to see a long struggle through, though little encouragement brightens their pathway?

COURAGEOUS FAITH

In the midst of a struggle that seems hopeless Jesus may have the greatest significance for us. He believed in God and his kingdom. He was willing to give his life for them unreservedly and unhesitatingly; and he did. Such a one can inspire *courageous faith* in us. The story of his life and death remains the greatest incentive we possess never to give up faith that God is an earnest Father of love. We should never belittle other ways to God, but if there is not a pathway here, where can it be found? Was the fourth evangelist mistaken, therefore, when he expressed his own faith through the lips of Jesus, "He that hath seen me hath seen the Father"?

How may this faith which Jesus evokes from us be rationally explained? It would be profitless for us to recount the story of the attempts of the theologians to show how Jesus was at the same time "very God of very God," and "very man of very man," and what were the eternal relations between the Father and the Son. Such expressions go far beyond our assured knowledge of Jesus. They also transcend any possible knowledge of God, and increasing numbers feel that they stand in no relation to actual religious experience and faith. Not a few earnest thinkers have sought to work out new formulas to express their faith that Jesus is the final revelation of God. While no one would check their zeal, we have no hopes in such explorations in metaphysics. Not that religion dare avoid ultimate questions, nor can she neglect to relate her thought to the rest of experience. An artificial isolation of religion can only cultivate a hothouse type of faith. But the relation of this one historical fact to the eternal world cannot be compressed in any formula.

At least for the average teacher of religion a different approach would seem to be more fruitful. Though this chapter has been devoted to modern *values* in Jesus, it should be abundantly clear that following him is tremendously difficult. A very natural question that comes to mind then is, "Why should I follow him?" Why should anyone undertake so difficult and impossible an undertaking? Waving aside all Christological theories, we may better turn to this question which can be answered from the world of our experience. If we say that we follow Jesus because we find in him the *most ultimate meaning* we can discover, no myths can add to his authority or increase the understanding of his person. If we have not discovered in him "the way, the truth, and the life," all the titles in the religious pantheon are nothing but empty words.

But for those who do make such a discovery Jesus may become more than an individual person. He may be a *symbol*. He sums up, as we have seen, the best in the heritage of Judaism. He has been the inspirer of much truth that he did not actually teach. In fact, many of the insights popularly ascribed to him are our own inspired by him. He becomes for many who love him a symbol of ultimate meaning. They can conceive nothing truer than a Christlike God.

The world still stands in desperate need of the good

news of a redeeming God upon whom we depend for life. Old interpretations in terms of Jewish messianism and ancient mysteries are no longer possible for men and women living in the twentieth century. But modern science and technology will not furnish us the motive power to launch out with the courageous faith that nevertheless this *is* our Father's world. We know of no greater inspiration to put to the test belief in a redeeming God of love than the Jesus who "loved us and gave himself for us." From the depths of our need, we too reply, "To whom shall we go? thou hast the words of eternal life."

SELECTED BIBLIOGRAPHY

1. *The Modern Study of the Bible*

   Dodd, C. H., *The Authority of the Bible*, 1929. Harpers.
   Fosdick, H. E., *The Modern Use of the Bible*, 1925. Macmillan.
   Jones, J. M., *The New Testament in Modern Education*, 1922. Hodder & Stoughton.
   Streibert, N. A., *Youth and the Bible*, 1924. Macmillan.

2. *The Study of Jesus*

   Easton, B. S., *Christ in the Gospels*, 1930. Scribners.
   Schweitzer, A., *The Quest of the Historical Jesus*, 1910. A. & C. Black.

3. *The Study of the Sources*

   Burton, E. D., and Willoughby, Harold, *A Short Introduction to the Gospels.*
   Easton, B. S., *The Gospel Before the Gospels*, 1928. Scribners.
   Streeter, B. H., *The Four Gospels*, 1925. Macmillan.
   Taylor, Vincent, *The Gospels*, 1930. Epworth.

4. *Modern Reconstructions of the Life of Jesus*

   Bosworth, E. I., *The Life and Teachings of Jesus*, 1924. Macmillan.
   Case, S. J., *Jesus* (liberal), 1927. University of Chicago.
   Headlam, A. C., *The Life and Teachings of Jesus, The Christ* (conservative), 1923. Oxford.
   Klausner, Jos., *Jesus of Nazareth* (Jewish), 1926. Macmillan.
   Mackinnon, James, *The Historic Jesus*, 1931. Longmans.
   Murry, J. M., *Jesus, Man of Genius* (literary), 1926. Harpers.

5. *The Teachings of Jesus*

Branscomb, Harvie, *The Teachings of Jesus*, 1931. Cokesbury.

Bundy, W. E., *The Religion of Jesus*, 1928. Bobbs-Merrill.

Bundy, W. E., *The Recovery of Jesus*, 1929. Bobbs-Merrill.

Burton, E. D., *A Source Book for the Study of the Teaching of Jesus*, 1923. University of Chicago.

Deissmann, A., *The Religion of Jesus and the Faith of Paul*, 1923. Doran.

Mathews, Shailer, *Jesus on Social Institutions*, 1928. Macmillan.

Robinson, B. W., *The Sayings of Jesus*, 1930. Harpers.

Scott, E. F., *The Ethical Teachings of Jesus*, 1924. Macmillan.

6. *Problems in the Life of Jesus*

Goguel, M., *Jesus the Nazarene—Myth or History*, 1926. Unwin.

Palmer, F., *The Virgin Birth*, 1924. Macmillan.

Taylor, V., *The Historical Evidence for the Virgin Birth*, 1920. Oxford.

Micklem, E. R., *Miracles and the New Psychology*, 1922. Oxford.

Wright, C. J., *Miracle in History and in Modern Thought*, 1929. Constable.

Robinson, W. H., *The Parables of Jesus*, 1928. University of Chicago.

Buttrick, George, *The Parables of Jesus*, 1928. Doubleday, Doran.

Gardner-Smith, P., *The Narratives of the Resurrection*, 1926. Methuen.

7. *Popular Treatments of Jesus.*

Anonymous, *By an Unknown Disciple*, 1919. Doran.

Fosdick, H. E., *The Manhood of the Master*, 1913. Association Press.

SELECTED BIBLIOGRAPHY

Glover, T. R., *The Jesus of History*, 1917. Association Press.

Simkovitch, V. G., *Toward the Understanding of Jesus.* Macmillan.

8. *The Interpretation of Jesus*

Andrews, H. T., and others, *The Lord of Life*, 1929. Macmillan.

Baillie, John, *The Place of Jesus Christ in Modern Christianity*, 1929. Scribners.

Bell, G. K. A., and Deissmann, A., *Mysterium Christi*, 1930. Longmans.

Loofs, Fr., *What Is the Truth About Jesus Christ?* 1913. Scribners.

Rawlinson, A. E. J., *The New Testament Doctrine of the Christ*, 1926. Longmans.

9. *Books for Children*

Danielson, Frances W., *The Bible Story Book*, 1924. Pilgrim Press.

Sherman, H. A., and Kent, C. F., *The Children's Bible*, 1922. Scribners.

Blanchard, F. Q., *How One Man Changed the World*, 1928. Pilgrim Press.

Hodges, George, *When the King Came*, 1912. Houghton, Mifflin.

Jones, Rufus, *The Boy Jesus and His Companions*, 1922. Macmillan.

Rihbany, A. M., *The Christ Story for Boys and Girls*, 1916. Houghton, Mifflin.

10. *Texts for Adolescents*

Buck, Florence, *The Story of Jesus*, 1917. Beacon.

Fiske, G. W., *Jesus' Ideals of Life*, 1922. Abingdon.

Forbush, *The Life of Jesus*. Scribners.

Grant, F. C., *The Life and Times of Jesus*, 1921. Abingdon.

Hunting, Harold, *A Life of Christ for Young People.* Minton, Balch & Co.

11. *Texts for Adults*

Curry, Bruce, Jr., *Jesus and His Cause*, 1926. Association Press.

Rall, H. F., *The Life of Jesus*, 1917. Abingdon.

Rall, H. F., *The Teaching of Jesus*, 1918. Abingdon.